M̶ ♡ S0-BEZ-303

MAUREEN!!

LOVE,

KELLEE

Algrove Publishing Limited
1090 Morrison Drive
Ottawa, Ontario
Canada K2H 1C2

National Library of Canada Cataloguing in Publication Data

Waterman, Catharine H. (Catharine Harbeson), b. 1812
   Flora's lexicon : an interpretation of the language and sentiment of flowers

(Classic reprint series)
Reprint of the ed. published: Boston : Crosby, Nicholas, Lee & Co., 1860.
ISBN 1-894572-42-4

   1. Flowers language. 2. Symbolism of flowers. I. Title. II. Series: Classic reprint series (Ottawa, Ont.)

GR780.W38 2001   398'.368213   C2001-900360-9

Printed in Canada
#10901

FLORA'S LEXICON:

AN

INTERPRETATION

OF

THE LANGUAGE AND SENTIMENT

OF

FLOWERS:

WITH

AN OUTLINE OF BOTANY,

AND A

POETICAL INTRODUCTION.

BY CATHARINE H. WATERMAN.

BOSTON:
CROSBY, NICHOLS, LEE & COMPANY.
1860.

ADVERTISEMENT.

THE language of flowers has recently attracted so much attention, that an acquaintance with it seems to be deemed, if not an essential part of a polite education, at least a graceful and elegant accomplishment. A volume furnishing a complete interpretation of those meanings most generally attached to flowers, has therefore become a desirable, if not an essential part of a gentleman's or a lady's library. In the manual now offered to the public, an attempt has been made to comprise all that is important in the way of interpretation in a reasonable compass, and to adorn this part of the work with such quotations from the best poets of our language, both native and foreign, as have a direct and graceful reference either to the peculiarities of the flowers, or to the sentiments which they are made to express. The outline of Botany placed at the end of the volume will be found to contain a sufficiently clear exposition of the Linnean system to explain fully the scientific terms and the classification used in the body of the work.

THE

LANGUAGE OF FLOWERS.

EARTH hath a thousand tongues, tha swell
    In converse soft, and low —
We hear them in the flowery dell,
    And where the waters flow.
We note them when the pliant reed
    Bends to the summer air,
Its low-toned music gently freed
    By the soft breezes there ;
And angels from their starry height,
On hills, and dales, and green banks write.

There is a language in each flower
    That opens to the eye,
A voiceless — but a magic power,
    Doth in earth's blossoms lie ;
The flowering Almond, first to bring
    Its perfume to the breeze,
The earliest at the call of spring,
    Among the green-clad trees,
Whispers of Indiscretion's fate,
Trusting too soon — convinced too late.

The Wall Flower clinging cheerfully,
    Amid decaying bloom,
Tells of the heart's fidelity,
    In stern misfortune's gloom;
And like the clasping Ivy vine,
    When all around depart,
Closer in storms the bonds entwine,
    Of friendship round the heart.
And glory's crown is proudly seen,
In the bright Laurel's evergreen.

Hope smiles amid the blossoms white
    That crown the Hawthorn bough,
And in the Myrtle's leaflets bright,
    Love softly breathes his vow.
The little Lily of the Vale
    Seems sent our hearts to bless,
Still whispering, on spring's balmy gale,
    Return of Happiness.
While blooming on some favour'd spot,
We trust to thee, Forget-me-not.

And quivering to the lightest wind
    That fans the summer flower,
The Aspen's tender leaves we find,
    Shrinking beneath its power,
At every trembling breath that steals
    Its spreading boughs between,
Each little blossom's leaf reveals
    A pang of misery keen;

Like lightly utter'd careless words,
Wounding the heart's half-broken chords.

Woe for the Aspen tree — and woe
  For hearts too finely strung,
The tempest wind shall round them blow,
  And heart — and branch, be wrung;
The storm's dread wing shall o'er them sweep,
  And bow them to the blast,
While each must early learn, to weep
  The hopes that could not last:
The bosom's sensibility,
Is pictured in the Aspen tree.

The little Blue Bell lifts its head
  The Amaryllis beside,
Emblems, upon their grassy bed,
  Of Lowliness and Pride,—
Bright as the summer's bluest cloud,
  Each opening Bell appears,
The sun, that gilds the floweret proud,
  Its humble blossom cheers;
Sweeter the Blue Bell's lowly mien,
Than Pride, in dazzling radiance seen.

The variegated Columbine
  Hangs its bright head to earth,
As half ashamed the sun should shine
  Upon its place of birth;

And drooping on its tender stem,
    As the low night-wind swells,
It seems in many a dew-drop gem,
    Like Folly's Cap, and Bells;
Rung by the wind in frolic play,
Whene'er they sportive pass that way.

The Musk Rose loads the evening breeze,
    With its own rich perfume,
Wafting far incense thro' the trees,
    From its thick clustering bloom;
Charming, as Beauty's palmiest hours,
    Capricious as its smiles,
One Summer sees it crown'd with flowers,
    The next no breezy wiles
Can lure one bud, where thousands smiled,—
And hence capricious Beauty styled.

And what is beauty? — lo, the sun
    That left the blooming spray,
Shines once again the boughs upon —
    The Roses — where are they?
Some strew with leaves the grassy plain,
    Flashing in crimson hue,
Some languish there, that ne'er again
    Shall drink the evening dew;
And fleeting Beauty's sadden'd close,
Is traced in the pale, wither'd Rose.

What brings the bright and shining leaf,
    The scarlet Poppy wears?
A consolation for our grief,
    A solace for our cares;
The ancients wreathed the brows of sleep,
    With the rich Poppy flowers,
For slumber dries the eyes that weep,
    And pictures happier hours;
And in its scarlet blossom rests
    A healing balm for wounded breasts.

Yes — flowers have tones — God gave to each
    A language of its own,
And bade the simple blossom teach
    Where'er its seeds are sown;
His voice is on the mountain's height
    And by the river's side,
Where flowers blush in glowing light,
    In Lowliness, or Pride;
We feel, o'er all the blooming sod,
It is the language of our God.

He spreads the earth an open book
    In characters of life,
All where the human eye doth look
    Seems with his glory rife;
He paints upon the burning sky
    In every gleaming star,
The wonder of his nomes on high,
    Shining to faith afar;

His voice is in the tempest's wrath,
And in the soft south zephyr's path.

For us, frail, feeble things of clay,
    Are all these beauties given,
The glorious, wide-spread orb of day,
    And the bright starry heaven;
The far-stretch'd waters, and the land,
    The mountain, and the plain,
These are the free gifts of his hand,
    And shall they plead in vain?
Rocks, hills, and flowers, their homage pay,
And shall we worship less than they?

No — from the green enamell'd sod
    Let the soul's praises rise,
The living temple of our God,
    Arch'd by his own blue skies.
There, let thy grateful praise be heard,
    There, let thy prayers be given,
And with the hymns of flower and bird,
    They shall ascend to heaven,
And sooner reach the eternal bowers
Breathed over beds of blushing flowers.

FLORA'S LEXICON.

CACIA. *Robinia Pseudacacia.* Class **17,** DIADELPHIA. Order: DECANDRIA. The savages of North America have consecrated the Acacia to the genius of chaste love; their bows are made from the incorruptible wood of this tree, their arrows are armed with one of its thorns. These fierce children of the forest, whom nothing can subdue, conceive a sentiment of delicacy; perhaps what they are unable to express by words, but they understand the sentiment by the expression of a branch of blooming Acacia. The young savage, like the city coquette, understands this seducing language perfectly. The Acacia is a native of North America, and received its name from the botanist, Robin.

PLATONIC LOVE.

Our rocks are rough, but smiling there
The *Acacia* waves her yellow hair,
Lonely and sweet, nor loved the less
For flowering in a wilderness——
Then come—thy Arab maid will be
The loved and lone *Acacia* tree.　　MOORE.

CACIA ROSE. *Robinia Hispida.* Class 17, Diadelphia. Order: Decandria. Art has produced nothing that may vie in freshness and in elegance of appearance with this beautiful flowering shrub; its inclining branches,—the gaiety of its verdure,—its clusters of rose-coloured flowers, like bows of ribands, hung on branches clothed with hairs of a reddish brown, never fail to excite admiration, and have combined to render it a proper emblem of elegance. Its appearance has been compared to that of an elegant female in her ball dress.

ELEGANCE.

The fairness of her face no tongue can tell,
For she the daughters of all women's race,
And angels eke, in beautie doth excel,
Sparkled on her from God's own glorious face,
And more increast by her own goodly grace,
That it doth far exceed all human thought,
Ne can on earth compared be to aught.

SPENSER.

There's no miniature
In her face, but is a copious theme,
Which would, discours'd at large of, make a volume.
What clear arch'd brows! what sparkling eyes. tne li.ies
Contending with the roses in her cheeks,
Who shall most set them off. What ruby lips:—
Or unto what can I compare her neck,
But to a rock of crystal? Every limb
Proportion'd to love's wish, and in their neatness
Add lustre to the richness of her habit.
Not borrow'd from it.

MASSINGER.

 DONIS. *Flos Adonis.* Class 13, POLY-ANDRIA. Order: POLYGYNIA. Adonis was killed, while hunting, by a boar. Venus, who, for his sake, had relinquished the joys of Cythera, shed tears for the fate of her favourite. They were not lost; the earth received them, and immediately produced a light, delicate plant, covered with flowers resembling drops of blood. Bright and transient flowers, too faithful emblems of the pleasures of life, ye were consecrated by Beauty herself to painful recollections!

PAINFUL RECOLLECTIONS.

Full twenty years have pass'd away, since thou, beloved one!
With darkening eye to heaven upraised, the last time bless'd
    thy son;
And meekly closing thy thin hands, with mine between them
    press'd,
Fled, with my name upon thy lips, to thine eternal rest.

My first, my last, my *only* friend!—if aught the ransom'd know
Of the dark thoughts and sinful deeds that stain the world below,
How hath thy gentle spirit grieved, as but a mother's can,
To see thy precepts to the boy, neglected by the man!

But no; thou art beatified!—on yonder radiant shore,
The sins and sorrows of thy child can trouble thee no more;
And if, in thy refulgent home, thou thinkest of me now,
'T is with my childhood's innocence yet beaming on my brow!

So would I have thee see thy son, the wreck'd of passion's storm,
With prematurely wrinkled brow, pale cheek, and stooping form,
To thy soul's gaze, immortal one! would ever present be,
The same fair child of guileless heart, that gamboll'd at thy knee.

                  THE KNICKERBOCKER.

 LMOND. *Amygdalus.* Class 12, Icosan-
dria. Order: Monogynia. Fable confers
an affecting origin on this tree. It relates
that Demophoon, son of Theseus and Phæ-
dra, in returning from the siege of Troy,
was thrown by a storm on the shores of
Thrace, where then reigned the beautiful
Phyllis. The young queen graciously received the prince, fell
in love with him, and became his wife. When recalled to Athens
by his father's death, Demophoon promised to return in a month,
and fixed the day. The affectionate Phyllis counted the hours
of his absence, and at last the appointed day arrived. Nine times
she repaired to the shore; but, losing all hope of his return, she
dropped down dead with grief, and was turned into an Almond-
tree. Three months afterwards, Demophoon returned. Over-
whelmed with sorrow, he offered a sacrifice at the sea-side, to
appease the manes of his bride. She seemed to sympathize with
his repentance: for the Almond-tree, into which she had been
transformed, instantly put forth its flowers, and proved by this
last effort that true love, " strong as death," is incapable of change.

INDISCRETION.

Like to an almond-tree, mounted high
On top of green Selinis, all alone,
With blossoms brave bedecked daintily;
Whose tender locks do tremble every one,
At every little breath that under heav'n is blown.

Spenser.

According to Moore, the Almond blossom is the emblem of
hope—

The hope, in dreams of a happier hour,
   That alights on Misery's brow,
Springs out of the silvery almond-flower,
   That blooms on a leafless bough.

In ancient times, the abundance of blossom on this tree was
considered as the promise of a fruitful season.

LOE. Class 6, HEXANDRIA. Order: Mo-NOGYNIA. The aloe is said to thrive best in the desert, and is only attached to the soil by a very slender fibre. Its taste is very sharp and bitter. So sorrow drives us away from the world, detaches our hearts from the earth, and fills them with bitterness. This plant derives its support almost entirely from the air, and assumes very singular and fantastic shapes. Le Vaillant found many species very numerous in the deserts of Namaquoise; some of them six feet long, which were thick and armed with long spines. From the centre of these a light twig shoots forth to the height of a tall tree, all garnished with flowers. Others exalt themselves like the cactus, bristling with thorns. Others, again, are marbled, and seem like serpents creeping upon the earth. Brydone saw the ancient city of Syracuse entirely covered by great aloes in flower; their elegant branches giving to the promontory which bounded the coast, the appearance of an enchanted forest. These plants also prosper well in our gardens. The collection in the museum of Paris is said to be the most complete in the world.

These magnificent and monstrous members of the vegetable kingdom are also found in barbarous Africa. There they grow upon the rocks in arid and sandy soil, in the midst of that burning atmosphere in which scarce aught but tigers and lions can breathe and live. Let us bless Providence, then, for raising in our climate verdant bowers over our heads, and for spreading under our feet the soft carpet of grass, ornamented with saffron, violets, and daisies.

GRIEF.

Besides, you know,
Prosperity's the very bond of love;
Whose fresh complexion, and whose heart together,
Affliction alters.
SHAKSPEARE.

MARANTH. *Amaranthus.* Class 21, Mo-NÆCIA. Order: PENTANDRIA. The ama-ranth is one of the latest gifts of autumn, and when dead its flowers retain their rich scarlet colour. The ancients have associ-ated it with supreme honours; choosing it to adorn the brows of their gods. Poets have sometimes mingled its bright hue with the dark and gloomy cypress, wishing to express that their sorrows were combined with everlasting recollections. Homer tells us, that at the fune-ral of Achilles, the Thessalians presented themselves wearing crowns of amaranth.

IMMORTALITY.

Milton, in his gorgeous description of the court of heaven, mentions the amaranth as being inwoven in the diadems of an-gels—

> With solemn adoration down they cast
> Their crowns, inwove with amaranth and gold;
> Immortal amaranth, a flower which once
> In Paradise, fast by the tree of life,
> Began to bloom; but soon for man's offence
> To heaven removed, where first it grew, there grows,
> And flowers aloft, shading the fount of life,
> And where the river of bliss through midst of heaven
> Rolls o'er Elysian flowers her amber stream,
> With those that never fade.

Pope mentions this flower in his Ode for St. Cecilia's day; imagining it to be found in celestial bowers;—

> By the streams that ever flow,
> By the fragrant winds that blow
> O'er the Elysian flowers;
> By those happy souls that dwell
> In yellow meads of asphodel,
> Or amaranthine bowers.

MERICAN COWSLIP. *Primula Veris.*
Class 5, PENTANDRIA. Order: MONOGY-
NIA. The elegant stem of a single root of
this plant springs from the centre of a ro-
sette of large leaves couched on the earth.
In April it is crowned with twelve pretty
flowers with the cups reversed. Linnæus
has given it the name of "Dodecatheon," which signifies "twelve
divinities," a name, perhaps, somewhat too extravagant for a
small plant so modest in its appearance. An American writer
says of them, in their indigenous soil, that they resemble a cluster of bright yellow polyanthuses. "Our gold cowslips," he
adds, "look like a full branch of large clustering king-cups; they
carelessly raise themselves on their firm stalks, their corollas
gazing upward to the changing spring sky, as they grow amidst
their pretty leaves of vivid green. They adorn almost every
meadow, and shed a glow of beauty wherever they spring."

YOU ARE MY DIVINITY.

At such an hour, thine image, brought
　By Memory to the passive eye,
Would blend with every gentle thought
　Of dwellers in the distant sky,
　And float, in airy seeming, by,
Fit princess of the sylphid crowds,
　Born of the wealth of Fantasy
In her own heaven of Summer clouds,
　Where ever laughing sunbeams shine
　On eyes as calm and bright as thine.
　　　　　　　　　J. R. CHORLEY.

——Cowslips wan that hang the pensive head.
　　　　　　　　　MILTON.

Anxious cares the pensive nymph opprest,
And secret passions labour'd in her breast.
　　　　　　　　　POPE.

MARYLLIS. *Amaryllis Sarniensis.* Class 6, HEXANDRIA. Order: MONOGYNIA. Gardeners say that the amaryllis, of which there are numerous varieties, is a proud plant, because it frequently refuses its flowers to their most earnest cares. The Guernsey lily is a charming flower, and closely resembles the tuberose in appearance and size; it is of a cherry red colour, and, when the sun shines upon it, it seems studded with gems of gold. The name of this plant is derived from a Greek word, which has been not inappropriately translated, by Monsieur Pirolle, as significant of splendour, and perhaps we have no flowering plant more beautifully gay than the amaryllis.

HAUGHTINESS. PRIDE.

——————But he his wonted *pride*
Soon recollecting, with high words, that bore
Semblance of worth, not substance, gently raised
Their fainting courage, and dispell'd their fears.
MILTON.

How poor a thing is pride! when all, as slaves,
Differ but in their fetters, not their graves.
DANIEL.

Pride by presumption bred, when at a height,
Encount'ring with contempt, both march in ire;
And 'twixt 'em bring base cruelty to light;
The loathsome offspring of a hated sire.
STERLINE.

I'll offer, and I'll suffer no abuse,
Because I'm proud; pride is of mighty use.
The affectation of a pompous name,
Has oft set wits and heroes in a flame:
Volumes, and buildings, and dominions wide,
Are oft the noble monuments of pride.
CROWN.

MERICAN ELM. *Ulmus Americana.* Class 5, PENTANDRIA. Order: DIGYNIA. The American Elm is found in all parts of the United States, but thrives best between the forty-second and forty-sixth degrees of north latitude. The wood is inferior to the European, and as it is in consequence not very well adapted to practical purposes, its uses are few and unimportant.

PATRIOTISM.

I see thee weep, and thine are honest tears,
A patriot's for his country. Thou art sad
At thought of her forlorn and abject state,
From which no power of thine can raise her up.

COWPER.

Give me the death of those
Who for their country die;
And O be mine like their repose,
When cold and low they lie!
Their loveliest mother earth
Enshrines the fallen brave;
In her sweet lap who gave them birth,
They find their tranquil grave.

MONTGOMERY.

In that dread hour my country's guard I stood,
From the state's vitals tore the coil'd serpent,
First hung with writhing up to public scorn,
Then flung him forth to ruin.

MATURIN.

O heaven! he cried, my bleeding country save!
Is there no hand on high to shield the brave?
Yet, though destruction sweep those lovely plains,
Rise, fellow men! our country yet remains!
By that dread name we wave the sword on high!
And swear for her to live! with her to die!

CAMPBELL.

MERICAN LINDEN, or BASS-WOOD. *Tilia Americana.* Class 13, POLYANDRIA. Order: MONOGYNIA. The American Linden, or Bass-wood, is a lofty tree, but the wood is not extensively used in the arts. We have two other species, in the south and west, whose wood possesses similar properties, and is likewise little employed.

MATRIMONY.

From that day forth, in peace and joyous bliss
They lived together long without debate;
Nor private jars, nor spite of enemies,
Could shake the safe assurance of their states.

SPENSER.

        Nothing shall assuage
Your love but marriage: for such is
The tyeing of two in wedlock, as is
The tuning of two lutes in one key: for
Striking the strings of the one, straws will stir
Upon the strings of the other; and in
Two minds link'd in love, one cannot be
Delighted, but the other rejoiceth.

LILLY.

Marriage is a matter of more worth,
Than to be dealt in by attorneyship.

SHAKSPEARE.

What is wedlock forced but a hell,
An age of discord and continual strife?
Whereas the contrary bringeth forth bliss,
And is a pattern of celestial peace.

SHAKSPEARE.

MERICAN ARBOR-VITÆ. *Thuja occidentalis.* Class 21, Monœcia. Order: Monadelphia. The American Arbor-vitæ is found in the same region as the spruces, where it is called White Cedar; and indeed it much resembles in its appearance the Cupressus Thugoides, or genuine White Cedar. It grows to the height of 50 or 60 feet, with the trunk 10 or 15 inches in diameter, and is now planted for ornament in all parts of the Union. The wood is soft, fine-grained, and is highly esteemed for its durability; but it is difficult to procure stalks of any considerable length with a uniform diameter.

IMMORTALITY.

Look nature through: 'tis revolution all;
All change; no death. Day follows night, and night
The dying day; stars rise, and set, and rise;
Earth takes th' example. See the summer gay,
With her green chaplet, and ambrosial flowers,
Droops into pallid autumn: winter grey,
Horrid with frost, and turbulent with storm,
Blows autumn and his golden fruits away,
Then melts into the spring: soft spring, with breath
Favonian, from warm chambers of the south,
Recalls the first. All, to re-flourish, fades;
As in a wheel, all sinks, to reascend.
Emblems of man, who passes, not expires.

Young.

Immortality o'ersweeps
All pains, all tears, all time, all fears—and peais
Like the eternal thunders of the deep
Into my ears this truth—Thou liv'st for ever.

Byron.

NEMONE. *Anemone.* Class 13, POLY-ANDRIA. Order: POLYGYNIA. Anemone was a nymph beloved by Zephyr. Flora, being jealous, banished her from her court, and changed her into a flower, which always opens at the return of spring. Zephyr had abandoned this unfortunate beauty to the rude caresses of Boreas, who, unable to gain her love, agitates her until her blossoms are half open, and then causes her immediately to fade. An anemone, with this motto, " *Brevis est usus,*"—" Her reign is short," admirably expresses the rapid decline of beauty.

FORSAKEN.

She will not speak the anguish of her breast,
    She cannot chide the one she loves to bless;
What though her bosom own no soothing rest?
    She does not cease to pray for his distress:
Her heart is wasting in a slow decay,
And the disease of hope smiles o'er her prey.

At times she wanders when the air is warm,
    And gazes on the trysting-place so dear,
When love and innocence, in gentle form,
    United like a dew-drop and a tear,
When happy thoughts went heavenward in sweet **prayer;**
And all was bliss when Waldron's smile was there.

And then she turns her sicken'd heart away,
    And bends her footsteps to her mother's grave.
Thinking how soon she'll mingle with her clay—
    She knows there is no human arm to save.
And though she smiles at death—her thoughts of life,
And faithless Waldron, cause a tearful strife.

DAWES.

NGELICA. *Angelica.* Class 5, PENTAN-DRIA. Order 2: DIGYNIA. This plant is named angelica in allusion to its agreeable smell and medicinal qualities. It has wing-ed leaves divided into large segments; its stalks are hollow and jointed, the flowers grow in an umbel upon the tops of the stalks, and consist of five leaves, succeeded by two large chan-nelled seeds. Archangelica is sometimes cultivated in gardens for its leaf-stalks, to be blanched and eaten as celery, or candied with sugar. In Lapland, where it is also found, it is used to crown poets, who fancy themselves inspired by its agreeable odour.

INSPIRATION.

My fancy form'd thee of angelic kind.
POPE.

Amid the burning stars of night I saw
A brighter glory — for thy spirit shone
Through the clear heavens all beautiful, alone,
And fill'd my heart with rapture and with awe.
I heard thy voice — blest who their Maker's law
Within their inmost soul in peace enthrone,
For this celestial world is all their own;
No earthly gaud hath ever power to draw
Downward their brighter gaze — Oh! be tnou one!
Thou whom I loved upon that lower scene,
Soar up and join me!—dark clouds swept between—
The stars were veil'd—the radiant light was gone—
Yet, Angel Spirit! when earth's shadows flee,
On hope's immortal wing I trust to follow thee.
ANON.

PPLE BLOSSOM. *Pyrus.* Class 12, PEN-TAGYNIA. Order: ICOSANDRIA. What is more enchanting to the lover of nature than the apple-tree when clad with its beautiful bloom in the early spring? and the more, that they hold forth the promise of an abundance of delicious fruit. The apple bloom is indeed a charming flower, and by some is preferred before the rose.

PREFERENCE.

The lasses aw wonder'd what Willy could see,
In yen that was dark and hard-featur'd like me
And they wonder'd ay mair when they talk'd o' my wit,
And slily telt Willy, that could'nt be it:
But Willy he laugh'd, and he made me his wife,
And whea was mair happy thro' aw his lang life?
Its e'en my great comfort, now Willy is geane,
That he often said, nea pleace was like his awn heame.

I mind when I carried my wark to yon stile,
Where Willy was dyking, the time to beguile,
He would fling me u daisy to put i' my breast,
And I hammer'd my noddle to make out a jest:
But merry or grave, Willy often would tell,
There was nin o' the lave that was like my awn sel;
And he spake what he thought, for I'd hardly a plack
When we married, and nobbet ae gown to my back.

When the clock had struck eight, I expected him heame,
And wheyles went to meet him as far as Dumleane;
Of aw hours it telt, *eight* was dearest to me,
But now when it strikes, there's a tear i' my e'e.
O Willy! dear Willy! it never can be,
That age, time, or death, can divide thee and me;
For that spot on the earth, that's aye dearest to me,
Is the turf that has cover'd my Willy frae me.

GILPIN.

 RBOR VITÆ, or TREE OF LIFE. *Thuja.* Class 21, Monœcia. Order: Monadelphia. *Thuja*, the name of a tree, whose very durable wood served, according to Theophrastus, to make images. Its roots, in particular, being curiously twisted or veined, were used for the most valuable ornamental works. This plant was probably the *Juniperus Oxycedrus*, very common throughout Greece and the Archipelago, of which it is supposed on good authority that the most ancient statues were made. Our present genus of *Thuja* has nothing in common with this classical plant, except being an aromatic evergreen tree of the same order, with very durable wood; but it is not a native of Greece or the Levant.

LIVE FOR ME.

"Hafed, my own beloved lord,"
She kneeling cries—"first, last adored!
If in that soul thou'st ever felt
  Half what thy lips impassion'd swore,
Here, on my knees, that never knelt
  To any but their God before,
I pray thee, as thou lovest me, fly,
Now, now—ere yet their blades are nigh.
Oh haste—the bark that bore me hither
  Can waft us o'er yon darkening shore,
East—west—alas, I care not whither,
So thou art safe and I with thee!
Go where ye will, this hand in thine,
  Those eyes before me smiling thus,
Through good and ill, through storm and shine,
  The world's a world of love for us!
On some calm, blessed shore we'll dwell,
Where 'tis no crime to love too well."

Moore.

SH. *Fraxinus.* Class 2, DIANDRIA. Order: MONOGYNIA. There is a singular allegory in the Edda, which states that the gods hold their court under the shade of a miraculous ash, whose extensive branches shadow the whole surface of the earth; the top of the tree touches the heavens, and its roots descend to the regions of Pluto. An eagle constantly reposes on the tree, to observe every thing, and a squirrel continually ascends and descends to make report. Beneath its roots flow two fountains. In the one wisdom is concealed, and in the other is found the knowledge of things to come. Three virgins are entrusted with the charge of this sacred tree, who ever remain under its branches to refresh the tree with these salutary waters, which, on falling back on the earth, form a dew that produces honey. This effect has been ingeniously compared to the results of inventive science.

GRANDEUR.

> Nay, I know not.
> There are some qualities that women have
> Which are less worthy, but which warm us more
> Than speaking of their virtues. I remember
> The fair Giovanna in her pride at Naples.
> Gods! what a light enveloped her! She left
> Little to shine in history—but her beauty
> Was of that order that the universe
> Seem'd govern'd by her motion. Men look'd on her
> As if her next step would arrest the world;
> And as the sea-bird seems to rule the wave
> He rides so buoyantly, all things around her—
> The glittering army, the spread gonfalon,
> The pomp, the music, the bright sun in heaven—
> Seem'd glorious by her leave.
>
> WILLIS.

 SPEN TREE. *Populus Tremulus.* Class 12, DIŒCIA. Order: POLYANDRIA. Popular tradition states that the cross was made from this tree, and that since the Passion of our Saviour, the leaves have never known rest. The vibratory motion of the leaves is indeed curious, and never fails to attract the attention of the observer. It arises from the length and slenderness of the footstalks to which they are attached.

EXCESSIVE SENSIBILITY.

Why tremble so, broad *aspen tree?*
Why shake thy leaves ne'er ceasing?
At rest thou never seem'st to be,
  For when the air is still and clear,
Or when the nipping gale increasing,
  Snakes from thy boughs soft twilight's tear,
Thou tremblest still, broad aspen tree,
And never tranquil seem'st to be.

ANON.

Our sensibilities are so acute,
The fear of being silent makes us mute.

COWPER.

The soul of music slumbers in the shell,
Till waked and kindled, by the master's spell;
And feeling hearts — touch them but lightly — pour
A thousand melodies unheard before !

ROGERS.

Oh ! life is a waste of wearisome hours,
Which seldom the rose of enjoyment adorns;
And the heart that is soonest awake to the flowers,
Is always the first to be touch'd by the thorns.

MOORE.

SPHODEL. *Tofieldia palustris.* Class 6, HEXANDRIA. Order: TRIGYNIA. The yellow and white species of this elegant plant are old inhabitants of our gardens, are of very easy culture, and increase rapidly. The latter species covers immense tracts of land in Apulia, and affords very good nourishment to the sheep. It was sacred to Proserpine, and anciently used in funeral ceremonies; and it was believed that beyond the Acheron, the shades of the departed walked in vast meadows of Asphodel, where they drank the waters of oblivion.

MY REGRETS FOLLOW YOU TO THE GRAVE.

Sometimes my vision pictures thee, as stooping from on high,
The light of love ineffable illumining thine eye;
Then soaring up, on snowy wings, that brighten as they rise,
I hear thy soft voice calling me to meet thee in the skies!

I know that this is but a dream; that I can never see
Thy spirit, until mine shall wear the garment of the free;
That 't is my own imaginings that visit me by night,
But surely heaven the image clothes with something of its
  light!

Yes, mother! in thy holy home, death's gloomy valley past,
A hope hath risen in my heart, that we shall meet at last;
There these faint glimmerings of day, from yonder sphere un-
  trod,
Shall be exchanged for perfect light—the effluence of GOD!
       THE KNICKERBOCKER.

Dull grave — thou spoil'st the dance of youthful blood,
Strik'st out the dimple from the cheek of mirth,
And ev'ry smirking feature from the face;
Branding our laughter with the name of madness.
      BLAIR.

URICULA. *Primula Auricula.* Class 5, PENTANDRIA. Order: MONOGYNIA. As all the most beautiful flowers that were known to the ancients, had been placed in the hieroglyphical language of plants, we had some difficulty in making a selection worthy of representing the delightful art of painting. But our choice has at length fallen on the "queen of the snowy Alps," as the fittest emblem.

PAINTING.

O thou who seated by the golden wave
   Of classic Tiber, stol'st the prismy hues
From the rich landscape that Italia gave,—
   CLAUDE! whose celestial genius could transfuse
Heaven's beauty into earth's, and both combine
   In those undying paintings only thine;

Could'st thou have travell'd to our western sky,
   And near'd the setting sun, whose vesture spreads
Its gold and purple, blent harmoniously;
   When Autumn chills the foliage, and sheds
O'er the piled leaves among the evergreen,
   All colours and all teints to grace the scene;

Thou would'st have shown that there are other climes
   Besides Ausonia's where the heart may gush
With overwhelming fulness, and at times
   Feel the deep influence of bland nature's hush,
When Evening steals in blushes to her West,
And clouds are in their marriage garments drest.

                             DAWES.

ZALEA, INDIAN. *Azalea Indica.* Class PENT-DECANDRIA. Order: MONOGYNIA. A very splendid species of Azalea, with large and rich scarlet flowers. chosen. on account of the gorgeous splendour of its flowers, as the suitable emblem of Romance.

ROMANCE.

The pipe, and song, with many a mingled shout,
Ring through the forest, as the Satyr-rout
Dance round the dragon-chariot of Romance:
Forth pricks the Errant Knight with rested lance:
Imps, Dæmons, Fays, in antic train succeed,
The wand'ring maiden, and the winged steed!
The muttering Wizard turns, with haggard look,
The bloody leaves of the accursed book,
Whilst Giants, from the gloomy castle-tow'r,
With lifted Bats of steel, more dreadful low'r!
Hence, at midnight, thou shalt stray,
Where dark Ocean flings its spray,
To hear o'er Heav'n's resounding arch
The Thunder-Lord begin his march!
Or mark the flashes, that present
Some far-off shatter'd monument;
Whilst along the rocky vale,
Red fires, mingled with the hail,
Run along upon the ground,
And the thunders deeper sound!
The loftier Muse, with awful mien,
Upon a lonely rock is seen!
Full is the eye that speaks the dauntless soul;
She seems to hear the gathering tempest roll
Beneath her feet: She bids an eagle fly,
Breasting the whirlwind, through the dark-red sky!
Or, with elated look, lifts high the spear,
As sounds of distant battles roll more near. BOWLES.

ALM. *Melissa.* Class 14, DIDYNAMIA. Order: GYMNOSPERMIA. The scientific name of this plant is Melissa, which is synonymous with the Greek word for bee, being derived from μελι, honey, which is sought for in these flowers with avidity. "The recent plant has the agreeable odour of lemons." "It was formerly prized as a corroborant in hypochondriacal and nervous affections." It is on account of the soothing qualities of the waters distilled from this plant that it has been made the emblem of sympathy.

SYMPATHY.

Is there who mocks at sacred Sympathy,
And owns a bosom from her dictates free?
Who never long'd to press unto his heart,
At the first glance, a friend, and never part?
Who the soft influence of a smile denies,
And the more melting power of tearful eyes?
Who an unconscious look, a word, a sigh,
Boasts his unhallow'd bosom can defy?
O never let him deem his soul was made
For holy hopes, and joys that never fade,
For pure delights, that love can only know,
And all the ties that cheer our hearts below:
The tender names of husband, brother, friend,
Ne'er to his breast their blissful sounds shall lend,
But cheerless, joyless, shall he live and die,
Nor claim in life a smile, in death a sigh!

M. A. J.

For love is a celestial harmony
Of likely hearts composed of stars concent,
Which join together in sweet *sympathy,*
To work each others' joy and true content.

SPENSER.

ALSAM. *Impatiens.* Class 5, PENTAN-DRIA. Order: MONOGYNIA. This plant, which is one of the most beautiful and delicate of popular annuals, is a native of East India, and forms a showy cone of carnation-like flowers finely variegated. It possesses the peculiar property of retaining, during the hottest months of summer, all its freshness and beauty, while many other plants are withered before they have flowered. It has been named Nolitangere and Impaties, from the curious fact that when the seeds are ripe, they are thrown with considerable force out of the capsules on their being slightly touched; on this account it has been made the emblem of impatience. The Turks use it to represent ardent love.

IMPATIENCE.

Oh! for thy wings, thou dove!
  Now sailing by with sunshine on thy breast;
That, borne like thee above,
  I too might flee away, and be at rest!

Oh! to some cool recess
  Take, take me with thee on the summer wind!
Leaving the weariness,
  And all the fever of this life behind.

The aching and the void
  Within the heart whereunto none reply,
The early hopes destroyed——
  Bird! bear me with thee thro' the sunny sky.
                    HEMANS.

     Send quick, and summon in the council
To see the crown imposed! Bianca dies!
My throne hangs on your speed! Fly!
               N. P. WILLIS.

ARBERRY. *Berberis Vulgaris.* Class 6, HEXANDRIA. Order: MONOGYNIA. The common barberry is abundant in many parts of the United States. Its close branches and thorns render it peculiarly fit for hedges, and its brilliant red berries are very ornamental to the fields which it encircles. These berries, worn in the hair, have been mistaken for coral ornaments. Preserved in sugar, they form a cheap but much valued dainty among the farmers of New England. The fruit of the barberry is so very acid that birds will seldom eat them. The tree is armed with thorns, and the flowers are so irritable, that at the slightest touch all the stamina close around the pistil. Thus this tree bears all the characteristics of persons whose temper is sharp and irritable.

SHARPNESS. SOURNESS OF TEMPER.

Happiness courts thee in her best array;
But, like a misbehaved and sullen wench,
Thou pout'st upon thy fortune and thy love:
Take heed, take heed, for such die miserable.

SHAKSPEARE.

He reads much;
He is a great observer, and he looks
Quite through the deeds of men: he loves no plays,
As thou dost, Antony; he hears no music:
Seldom he smiles; and smiles in such a sort,
As if he mock'd himself, and scorn'd his spirit
That could be moved to smile at any thing.

SHAKSPEARE.

She is peevish, sullen, froward,
Proud, disobedient, stubborn, lacking duty;
Neither regarding that she is my child,
Nor fearing me as if I were her father.

SHAKSPEARE.

ASIL. *Ocimum Basilicum.* Class 14, Dɪ-
ᴅʏɴᴀᴍɪᴀ. Order: Gʏᴍɴᴏsᴘᴇʀᴍɪᴀ. Poverty is sometimes represented under the
figure of an old woman covered with rags,
seated near a plant of basil. It is commonly
said, that hate has the eyes of a basilisk,
because this name has been given to a fabu-
lous animal, which is stated to produce death by a single glance.
Basil, however, is a name derived from the Greek, which signifies royal, and indicates the excellence of this fragrant plant.

HATRED.

I had much rather see
A crested dragon, or a basilisk;
Both are less poison to my eyes and nature.

Dʀʏᴅᴇɴ.

No voice of friendly salutation cheer'd him,
None wish'd his arms might thrive, or bade God speed him:
But through a staring ghastly-looking crowd,
Unhail'd, unblest, with heavy heart he went.

Rᴏᴡᴇ.

Oh, that I could but mate him in his might,
Oh, that we were on the dark wave together,
With but one plank between us and destruction,
That I might grasp him in these desperate arms,
And plunge with him amid the weltering billows,
And view him gasp for life.

Mᴀᴛᴜʀɪɴ.

They did not know how hate can burn
In hearts once changed from soft to stern;
Nor all the false and fatal zeal
The convert of revenge can feel.

Bʏʀᴏɴ.

AY-BERRY, or WAX-MYRTLE. *Myrica cerifera.* Class 22, DIŒCIA. Ordei : TETRANDRIA. The Bay-berry, or Wax-myrtle, is a shrub found in the Northern and Middle Atlantic States, growing chiefly in barren soils. The name is derived from a waxlike substance, of a greenish colour and pleasant odour, which is obtained from the berries, and in some districts very abundantly.

INSTRUCTION.

She taught the child to read, and taught so well,
That she herself, by teaching, learn'd to spell.
BYRON.

'T is pleasing to be school'd in a strange tongue
By female lips and eyes — that is, I mean
When both the teacher and the taught are young,
As was the case at least where I have been ;
They smile so when one 's right, and when one 's wrong
They smile still more, and then there intervene
Pressure of hands, perhaps even a chaste kiss ;
I learn'd the little that I know by this.
BYRON.

Culture's hand
Has scatter'd verdure o'er the land ;
And smiles and fragrance rule serene,
Where barren wild usurp'd the scene.
And such is man — a soil which breeds
Or sweetest flowers, or vilest weeds ;
Flowers lovely as the morning's light,
Weeds deadly as an aconite ;
Just as his heart is train'd to bear
The poisonous weed, or flow'ret fair.
BOWRING.

BAY. *Laurus Nobilis.* Class 9, ENNEAN-DRIA. Order: MONOGYNIA. The Laurus Nobilis, or Sweet Bay, though but a shrub in our country, in Asia and the southern parts of Europe, its proper birth-place, attains to the height of twenty or thirty feet. It grows very freely on the banks of the river Peneus, in Thessaly; and hence, perhaps, the fable of the metamorphosis of Daphne, daughter of that river. It also, with classic propriety, adorns mounts Ida and Athos.

REWARD OF MERIT.

Not around the peaceful bower
  Should thy verdant branches twine,
Though thy leaves through wintry hour
  With unchanging lustre shine:
There are fitter scenes than this for thy bloom
  On the poet's lofty brow
  Let thy classic garlands glow,
  Or, if he lieth low,
    On his tomb.

Or, return'd from well-fought field,
  When the victor throws aside
Both his dinted helm and shield
  And his sword in crimson dyed,
O'er his trophies let thy green branches wave;
  For what so fit a meed
  From the country he has freed,
  As the laurel-wreath decreed
    To the brave?

                  ANON.

BEE ORCHIS. *Orchis.* Class 19, SYNGE-NESIA. Order: MONOGYNIA. This plant is singularly beautiful in its appearance, which so much resembles the bee, that it is frequently mistaken for one resting on the plant. It commonly grows near woods, and in the open meadows. The most successful method of cultivation is by choosing a soil and situation as natural to them as possible, and by suffering the grass to grow around them.

ERROR.

Well boots it the thick-mantled leas
To traverse: if boon nature grant,
To crop the insect seeming plant,
The vegetable Bee; or nigh
Of kin, the long-horn'd Butterfly,
White, or his brother purple pale,
Scenting alike the evening gale;
The Satyr flower, the pride of Kent,
Of Lizard-form, and goat-like scent.

BISHOP MANT.

O hateful Error, Melancholy's child!
Why dost thou show to the apt thoughts of men
The things that are not? O error, soon conceived,
Thou never com'st unto a happy birth,
But kill'st the mother that engender'd thee.

SHAKSPEARE.

When people once are in the wrong,
Each line they add is much too long;
Who fastest walks, but walks astray,
Is only furthest from his way.

PRIOR.

EECH. *Fagus Sylvatica.* Class 21, Monœcia. Order: Polyandria. To admire
the beech, is to rebel against high authority; yet who, that is not entirely devoted
to pictorial effect, but must admire it? The
oak may excel it in dignity, the elm in
beauty, and the ash in gracefulness: still
the beech is a noble tree; and in spring, the bright sunny tint
of its feathery foliage renders it a most attractive object.

WEDDED LOVE.

I have been wandering in the wood
   Where wither'd leaves my path were strewing;
And winds, with ire but half subdued,
   Seem'd to a future tempest growing.

Yet, 'mid these symbols of decay,
   My mind was only tuned to gladness:
And why?—It is our wedding day;
   What, then, have I to do with sadness?

I sat me down beneath a tree,—
   That tree, so famed for lover's ditty,
When he would try by each fond plea
   To move his mistress' soul to pity.

So smooth the sylvan tablet shone,
   So temptingly 't was spread before me,
I could not choose but trace thereon,
   No lover's, but a matron's story.

Yet ne'er did love, when hope and youth
   Each minister unto his pleasure,
Feel more of tenderness and truth
   Than I, whilst breathing this fond measure.

Long years ago, and side by side,
   We two were at the altar kneeling;
And whilst on earth the knot was tied,
   Angels, in heaven, our vows were sealing.

Anon.

ELL-FLOWER, ROUNDLEAVED BELL-FLOWER, or HAREBELL. *Campanula Rotundifolia.* Class 5, PENTANDRIA. Order: MONOGYNIA. The name of Bell-flower was never more appropriately bestowed than on this pretty, delicate plant, which has been imagined by some fanciful poets to ring out a peal of fairy music.

CONSTANCY.

Over the moorland, over the lea,
Dancing airily, there are we:
Sometimes, mounted on stems aloft,
   We wave o'er broom and heather,
To meet the kiss of the Zephyr soft;
   Sometimes, close together,
Tired of dancing, tired of peeping,
Under the whin you'll find us sleeping.

Daintily bend we our honey'd bells,
While the gossiping bee her story tells,
And drowsily hums and murmurs on
Of the wealth to her waxen storehouse gone,
And though she gathers our sweets the while,
We welcome her in with a nod and a smile.
TWAMLEY.

Sooner I'll think the sun would cease to cheer
The teeming earth, and then forget to bear;
Sooner that rivers would run back, or Thames
With ribs of ice in *June* would bind his streams:
Or nature, by whose strength the world endures,
Would change her course before you alter yours.
JONSON.

When all things have their trial, you shall find
Nothing is constant but a virtuous mind.
SHIRLEY.

IRCH. *Betula Alba.* Class 21, MONŒCIA. Order: POLYANDRIA. There is an elegance in the general appearance of the birch which fully justifies the poet's fancy, and entitles it to the appellation he has given it, of " Lady of the Woods." In every season, and under all circumstances, it is a lovely object; nothing can exceed the tender hue of its vernal leaves, as they wave to and fro in the sunshine. In summer, perhaps, it loses something of its beauty, as its bright tints then subside into a more sober green; still it preserves its gracefulness of aspect. In autumn it almost more than regains what it lost in summer; whilst winter, which deprives most other vegetable productions of their charms, by displaying more fully the slight silvery stem and delicate ramifications of the birch, seems but to invest it with new attractions.

GRACEFULNESS.

O! come to the woodlands, 't is joy to behold
The new-waken'd buds in our pathway unfold;
For spring has come forth, and the bland southern breeze
Is telling the tale to the shrubs and the trees,
  Which, anxious to show her
  The duty they owe her,
Have deck'd themselves gaily in em'rald and gold.

But though beautiful each, sure the fairest of all
Is yon *birch*, that is waving so graceful and tall:
How tender yet bright is the tint that is flung
O'er its delicate spray, which so lightly is hung,
  That like breeze of the mountain,
  Or gush of the fountain,
It owns not of rest or of slumber the thrall.

ANON.

IRD-CHERRY. *Prunus Padus.* Class 12, ICOSANDRIA. Order: MONOGYNIA. The bird-cherry is indigenous in most parts of Europe; it even opens its fragile flowers to the nipping air of Russia and Siberia. It abounds in the northern counties of England, and is profusely scattered among the woods, and on the borders of the mountain torrents of Scotland. In these natural fastnesses, where it is more likely to escape the stroke of the axe, it often rises to the height of fifteen feet from a stem eighteen inches in diameter, and spreads its branches to a considerable distance.

HOPE.

Time was, when shadowy eve
　　Was dearer to my heart than smiling morn,
And than the lovely garlands Spring doth weave,
　　The faded hues by pensive Autumn worn.

'T was in my youthful prime,
　　When life itself put on the look of Spring;
Ere Care, that ever tracks the steps of Time,
　　Seem'd other than a visionary thing.

Untouch'd by real grief,
　　E'en from its own excess of joy, my heart
In fancied ills would ofttimes seek relief,
　　And sport with Sorrow's yet unvenom'd dart.

But now, when every sigh
　　Is fraught, alas! with meaning full and deep;
When Hope resigns her seat to Memory,
　　And leaves me o'er her vanish'd dreams to weep:

Oh! now I turn away
　　From Autumn's sered wreaths to Spring's gay bloom;
Those all too sadly mind me of decay,
　　These bid sweet Hope once more her sway resume.
　　　　　　　　　　　　　　　　　ANON.

IRD'S-FOOT TREFOIL. *Lotos.* Class **17,** DIADELPHIA. Order: DECANDRIA. There are many species of the Bird's-Foot Trefoil. The most common *Lotos Corniculatus* is found in open grassy pastures, where it enlivens the Autumn, with its golden yellow flowers, striped with dark red. Its stem is clothed with close-pressed hairs, and its seed-vessel is copper-coloured. It is recommended for fodder for cattle, by the name of *Milk Vetch.*

REVENGE.

One sole desire, one passion now remains,
To keep life's fever still within his veins —
Vengeance! dire vengeance on the wretch who cast
O'er him and all he loved that ruinous blast.
For this he still lives on, careless of all
The wreaths that glory on his path lets fall;
For this alone exists — like lightening fire
To speed one bolt of vengeance, and expire!

MOORE.

Man spurns the worm, but pauses ere he wake
The slumbering venom of the folded snake:
The first may turn — but not avenge the blow;
The last expires — but leaves no living foe;
Fast to the doom'd offender's form it clings,
And he may crush — not conquer — still it stings!

BYRON.

How stands the great account 'twixt me and vengeance!
Tho' much is paid, yet still it owes me much;
And I will not abate a single groan.

YOUNG.

Had all his hairs been lives, my great revenge
Had stomach for them all.

SHAKSPEARE.

LUE-BOTTLE. *Centaurea Cyanus.* Class 19, SYNGENESIA. Order: FRUSTRANEA. The beautiful blue of this flower, which is of the colour of an unclouded sky, has made it the emblem of a tender and delicate sentiment, nourished by hope. According to ancient fable, this plant was called Cyanus, after a youth of that name, whose attachment to corn-flowers was so strong, that he employed his time chiefly in making garlands of them, seldom leaving the fields so long as his favourite flower was to be found, and always dressing himself in the fine blue colour of the flower he so much admired. Flora was his goddess; and, of all her gifts, this was the one he most admired. At last the youth was found dead in a corn-field, in the midst of a quantity of blue-bottles he had gathered. Soon after Flora transformed his body into this flower, in token of the veneration he had for her divinity.

DELICACY.

Thou wilt, I trust, find other hearts to bless,
And other verdant spots in life's dull waste,
And if my years roll on in loneliness,
Still I must tarry where my lot is cast, —
A martyr-task perchance — but not the less
Will I fulfil it — it must end at last,
And I will strive on other hearts to pour
The gifts of gladness mine may know no more!
I am but what I was before we met —
Beloved by some because my face is fair,
Because my brow throbs 'neath a coronet,
Because my brother is Ferrara's heir, —
But still in solitude I must forget
That one has known my inmost thoughts to share:
I must return amid the reckless throng,
To the deep silence I have nursed so long.

ANON.

ONUS HENRICUS, or GOOSEFOOT. *Chenopodium.* Class 5, PENTANDRIA. Order: DIGYNIA. The French people have given the name of their beloved king, Henry IV., to a beneficent and useful plant, which grows for the poor, and indeed seems exclusively to belong to them. In France it flourishes without any cultivation, and forms the asparagus and spinach of the poor; in England it is known also as wild spinach. The leaves are said to be of great service when applied to wounds. Happy is that king who deserves an homage so universal and so simple!

GOODNESS.

Whose nature is so far from doing harms,
That he suspects none.

SHAKSPEARE.

God's benison go with you; and with those
That would make *good* of bad, and friends of foes!

SHAKSPEARE.

———— He was too *good* to be
Where ill men were; and was the best of all
Amongst the rar'st of good ones.

SHAKSPEARE.

A most incomparable man; breathed, as it were,
To an untirable and continuate *goodness.*

SHAKSPEARE.

So far as May doth other months exceed,
So far in virtue and in *goodlihead*
Above all other nymphs Tanathe bears the meed.

THOMSON.

Your very goodness and your company
O'erpays all I can do.

SHAKSPEARE

OX. *Buxus.* Class 21, MONŒCIA. Order: TETRANDRIA. This tree is made symbolical of a Stoic, on account of the firmness of its wood, which, like the Stoics of old, cannot be warped. The box was formerly a favourite ornament for gardens, being planted in hedges and borders, which were trimmed into fantastical forms.

STOICISM. CONSTANCY.

O foolishness of men! that lend their ears
To those budge doctors of the *stoic* fur,
And fetch their precepts from the cynic tub,
Praising the lean and sallow abstinence.
MILTON.

How goodly looks Cytorus, ever green,
With *boxen* groves.
DRYDEN.

Nor box, nor limes, without their use are made,
Smooth-grain'd and proper for the turner's trade;
Which curious hands may carve, and seal
With ease invade.
VIRGIL.

I have won
Thy heart, my gentle girl! but it hath been
When that soft eye was on me; and the love
I told beneath the evening influence,
Shall be as *constant* as its gentle star.
WILLIS.

Why have I not this *constancy* of mind,
Who have so many griefs to try its force.
ADDISON.

Proud of her birth (for equals he had none),
The rest she scorn'd, but hated him alone;
His gifts, his constant courtship, nothing gain'd,
For she, the more he loved, the more disdain'd.
DRYDEN.

ROOM. *Genista.* Class 17, DIADELPHIA. Order: DECANDRIA. We presume that this plant has been made the emblem of neatness from the uses to which it is constantly applied. In our country villages, and throughout the country, it is known to every thrifty housewife as affording besoms for sweeping, whence originated the name of "broom" for those domestic cleansers.

There are many useful species of it. "The broom," says Mr. Martyn, "converts the most barren spot into an odoriferous garden."

NEATNESS.

On me such beauty summer pours,
That I am cover'd o'er with flowers;
And when the frost is in the sky,
My branches are so fresh and gay,
That you might look at me and say,
This plant can never die.
The butterfly, all green and gold,
To me hath often flown,
Here in my blossoms to behold
Wings lovely as his own.

WORDSWORTH.

Hypericum, all bloom, so thick a swarm
Of flowers, like flies, clothing her slender rods,
That scarce a leaf appears; mezereon too,
Though leafless, well attired, and thick beset
With blushing wreaths, investing every spray;
Althea, with the purple eye; the broom,
Yellow and bright, as bullion unalloyed
Her blossoms.

COWPER.

Sweet blooms genista in the myrtle shade.

DARWIN.

RYONY. *Bryonea Dioicia.* Class 21, Mo-
NŒCIA. Order: TRIANDRIA. The name
Bryony, and the botanical one, *Bryonea*, are
derived from a Greek word meaning to push
forth, or grow rapidly. The root grows to
an enormous size; in former times of ignorance and superstition, cunning impostors
made use of it in their pretended miraculous doings, and sometimes artfully contrived to make the root grow sufficiently like
the human figure to be supposed a magical resemblance. They
effected this by placing a mould of the shape required round the
roots of a healthy young Bryony plant, fastened with wires; and
such is the rapid growth of the root, that the image would be
formed in one summer.

PROSPERITY.

The slender Bryony that weaves
His pale green. flowers and glossy leaves
Aloft in smooth and lithe festoons;
And crown'd compact with yellow cones,
'Mid purple petals dropp'd with green,
The woody nightshade climbs between.

MANT.

———— Nightshade's purple flowers,
Hanging so sleepily their turban'd heads,
Rested upon the hedge; and *Bryony,*
So lavish of its vinelike growth, o'erhung
And canopied the flowers; while soften'd gleams
Of sunlight, falling through the leafy screen,
Shed a faint emerald tinge upon them all.

TWAMLEY.

Prosperity doth bewitch men, seeming clear;
But seas do laugh, show white, when rocks are near.

WEBSTER.

UTTER-CUP. *Ranunculus Æris.* Class 13, POLYANDRIA. Order: POLYGYNIA. This plant contains many virulent qualities, which are said to affect cattle, especially sheep, and particularly the root, which has the property of inflaming and blistering the skin. Shakspeare mentions it as the cuckoo-flower in King Lear,—

> Nettles, cuckoo-flowers,
> Darnell, and all the wild weeds.

And Clare, the Northamptonshire poet, alludes to its ungrateful qualities in some lines on the "Eternity of Nature:" detailing his morning's walk, he says,

> I wander out and rhyme;
> What hour the dewy morning's infancy
> Hangs on each blade of grass and every tree,
> And sprents the red thighs of the humble bee,
> Who 'gins betimes unwearied minstrelsy;
> Who breakfasts, dines, and most divinely sups,
> With every flower save golden buttercups,—
> On whose proud bosoms he will never go,
> But passes by with scarcely 'how do ye do,'
> Since in their showy, shining, gaudy cells,
> Haply the summer's honey never dwells.

INGRATITUDE.

> I served thee fifteen hard campaigns,
> And pitch'd thy standards in these foreign fields;
> By me thy greatness grew; thy years grew with it,
> But thy ingratitude outgrew them both.
>
> DRYDEN.

> He that's ungrateful, has no guilt but one;
> All other crimes may pass for virtues in him.
>
> YOUNG.

> He that doth public good for multitudes,
> Finds few are truly grateful.
>
> MARSTON.

AMELLIA, or JAPAN ROSE. *Camellia Japonica.* Class 16, MONADELPHIA. Order: POLYANDRIA. This splendid genus of flowers received its name from Geo. Joseph Kamel, whose name is written *Camellus* in Latin, a Jesuit, writer of a botanical work. It was introduced into England about the middle of last century, and has become a great favourite with florists, both in that country and the United States. There are many very splendid varieties to be found in the gardens and conservatories of Philadelphia.

MY DESTINY IS IN YOUR HANDS.

In pleasure's dream or sorrow's hour,
In crowded hall or lonely bower,
The business of my soul shall be,
For ever to remember thee !

MOORE.

Oh magic of love ! unembellish'd by you
Has the garden a blush or the herbage a hue ?
Or blooms there a prospect in nature or art,
Like the vista that shines through the eye to the heart ?

MOORE.

That happy minglement of hearts,
Where, chang'd as chemic compounds are,
Each with its own existence parts,
To into a new one, happier far !

MOORE.

Oh what, while I could hear and see
Such words and looks, was heaven to me ?
Though gross the air on earth I drew,
'Twas blessed, while she breath'd it too;
Though dark the flowers, though dim the sky,
Love lent them light, while she was nigh.

MOORE.

ANTERBURY BELL. *Campanula Medium.* Class 5, PENTANDRIA. Order: MONOGYNIA. This was a very fashionable plant some thirty years ago, and is still cultivated. It is used in Holland as an ornament to halls and staircases, and for placing before fireplaces in the summer. For this purpose it is planted in large pots, and is trained in such a manner as to cover a large surface, and continues to flower for two or three months in shady places. When in full flower it is a very magnificent plant, rising in a pyramidal shape, not unlike that of the towering pagoda. It may be trained to almost any shape, and we presume that on this account it has been made the emblem of gratitude.

GRATITUDE.

The benefits he sow'd in me, met not
Unthankful ground, but yielded him his own
With fair increase; and I still glory in it.
MASSINGER.

I find a pious gratitude disperse
Within my soul; and every thought of him
Engenders a warm sigh within me, which,
Like curls of holy incense, overtake
Each other in my bosom, and enlarge
With their embrace his sweet remembrance.
SHIRLEY.

I have five hundred crowns,
The thrifty hire I saved under your father,
Which I did store, to be my foster nurse,
When service should in my old limbs lie lame,
And unregarded age in corners thrown;
Take that: and He that doth the ravens feed,
Yea providently caters for the sparrow,
Be comfort to my age.
SHAKSPEARE.

ARDINAL'S FLOWER. *Lobelia Cardinalis.* Class 5, PENTANDRIA. Order: MONOGYNIA. This elegant plant is decorated with bright scarlet flowers. It is indigenous in our country, growing on the borders of rivers and streamlets. It is a flower of singular elegance and richness.

DISTINCTION.

For places in the court, are but like beds
In the hospital; where this man's head lies
At that man's foot, and so lower and lower.
WEBSTER.

If on the sudden he begins to rise;
No man that lives can count his enemies.
MIDDLETON.

All preferment
That springs from sin and lust shoots up quickly;
As gard'ner's crops do in the rott'nest grounds;
So is all means raised from base prostitution,
Even like a salad growing upon a dunghill.
MIDDLETON.

What throngs of great impediments besiege
The virtuous mind? so thick, they jostle
One another as they come. Hath vice a
Charter got, that none must rise, but such, who
Of the devil's faction are? the way to
Honour is not evermore the way to
Hell: a virtuous man may climb. Let the
Flatterer sell his lies elsewhere, it is
Unthrifty merchandise to change my gold
For breath.
DAVENANT.

ARNATION. *Dianthus.* Class 10, DECAN-
DRIA. Order: MONOGYNIA. We hope that
disdain is as scarce among our countrywomen as the yellow carnation is in our native
land. As disdainful people generally exact
homage, and possess little amiability; so
with this plant, it is the least beautiful and
fragrant of its kind, yet requires continual care and attention.

DISDAIN.

So proud she shineth in her princely state,
  Looking to heaven; for earth she did *disdain*,
And sitting high; for lowly she did hate:
  Lo, underneath her scornful feet was lain,
  A dreadful dragon with an hideous train.
SPENSER.

But shall the blood of her that loves me then
  Be sacrificed to her *disdainfulness*
That scorns my love? And shall I hope to win
  Mercy from her by being merciless?
DANIEL.

In vain he thus attempts her mind to move,
With tears and prayers, and late repenting love,
Disdainfully she look'd; then turning round,
But fix'd her eyes unmoved upon the ground.
DRYDEN.

There dwelt the scorn of vice, and pity too,
For those that did what she disdain'd to do,
So gentle and severe, that what was bad,
At once her hatred and her pardon had
WALLER.

There clamours with disdain the Scylla heard;
Much grudg'd the praise, but more the robb'd reward.
DRYDEN.

 HERRY TREE. *Prunus Cerasus.* Class 12, ICOSANDRIA. Order: MONOGYNIA. It is generally believed that the cherry tree was first introduced into Italy, 73 A. C., by Lucullus, who obtained it from a town in Pontus, in Asia, called Cerasus, whence it derives its specific name. The Romans brought it to England, though it is supposed that these have all been lost. There is no proof that cherries were in England at the period of the Norman conquest, nor for some time after; but Lydgate, who wrote about 1415, or before, says that cherries were then exposed for sale in the London market, as they are now in the early season. It is a very ornamental tree in the shrubbery and in woods, and is esteemed valuable, as encouraging the various species of thrush. We, of course, received it from Europe.

GOOD EDUCATION.

Nurse of my country's infancy, her stay
In youthful trials and in danger's day;
Diffusive Education! 'tis to thee,
She owes her mountain-breath of Liberty;
To thee she looks, through Time's illusive gloom,
To light her path, and shield her from the tomb;
Beneath thine Ægis, tyranny shall fail,
Before thy frown the traitor's heart shall quail;
Ambitious foes to liberty may wear
A patriot mask, to compass what they dare,
And sting the thoughtless nation, while they smile
Benignantly and modestly the while;
But thou shalt rend the virtuous-seeming guise,
And guard her from the worst of enemies.

　　　　　　　　　　　　　DAWES.

HINA, or INDIAN PINK. *Dianthus.* Class 10, DECANDRIA. Order: DIGYNIA. This gaily painted flower we have taken from the fertile soil of the east to decorate our parterres. Its colours are richer than those of the Sweet William, and it continues in flower for a longer period; but its flowers being placed singly on branching stems, like those of the common pink, they never present that fine mass of colour which the large umbel of the Sweet William exhibits, and they are entirely deficient in that fragrance for which the pink is so much admired.

AVERSION.

They say all breathing nature has an instinct
Of that which would destroy it. I of thee
Feel that abhorrence! If a glistering serpent
Hiss'd in my path, I could not shudder more,
Nor would I kill it sooner — so begone!
I'll strike thee dead else!

WILLIS.

Ask not which passion in my soul was higher,
My last *aversion*, or my first desire;
Nor this the greater was, nor that the less;
Both were alike, for both were in excess.

DRYDEN.

Sooner the olive shall provoke
To am'rous clasps this sturdy oak,
And doves in league with eagles be,
Ere I will glance a smile on thee.
Sooner yon duskish mulberry
In her old white shall clothed be,
And lizards with fierce asps combine,
Ere I will twist my soul with thine.

HALL.

HINA ASTER, or STARWORT. *Aster Chinensis.* Class 19. SYNGENESIA. Order: POLYGAMIA SUPERFLUA. Europe and America are indebted to the missionary, Father d'Incarville, for this beautiful various-coloured flower; he having first sent it to the "Jardin du Roi," at Paris, about 1730. At first it produced only simple flowers of one uniform colour; but, by cultivation, they became so doubled and quadrupled in form, and so varied in colour that it now forms one of the principal ornaments of the parterre, from July to November.

The Chinese, who have favoured us with this plant, make admirable use of it in decorating their gardens. To prepare them, they first raise the plants in pots; then, separating the colours, they dispose them with such infinite art as to produce one splendid and harmonious whole. This effect is often increased by planting them near the side of a lake.

The China-aster is made the emblem of variety; and owes its principal charms to a careful culture of the skilful gardener, who has surrounded its golden disks with every colour of the rainbow. So study produces an endless variety in the refinement of the human mind. Though majestic and brilliant, the China-aster is not the imprudent rival of the rose, but succeeds it, and consoles us for its absence.

VARIETY OF CHARMS.

Who hath not proved how feebly words essay
To fix one spark of beauty's heavenly ray?
Who doth not feel, until his failing sight
Faints into dimness with its own delight,
His changing cheek, his sinking heart confess
The might — the majesty of loveliness?

BYRON.

Heart on her lips, and soul within her eyes,
Soft as her clime, and sunny as her skies.

BYRON.

HRYSANTHEMUM, CHINESE. *Chrys-anthemum Indicum.* Class 19, SYNGENE-SIA. Order: SUPERFLUA. Cheerfulness is the best shield that can be found to lighten the strokes of adversity. This flower, that gives so much cheerfulness to the parterre, when nearly all the other children of Flora have withdrawn their smiles, is presented as the emblem of this enviable disposition, and of the loveliness which it adorns.

LOVELINESS AND CHEERFULNESS.

Smooth flow the waves, the zephyrs gently play,
Belinda smiled and all the world was gay.
POPE.

When Cheerfulness, a nymph of healthiest hue,
Her bow across her shoulders flung,
Her buskins gemm'd with morning dew,
Blew an inspiring air, that dale and thicket rung.
COLLINS.

And her against sweet cheerfulness was placed,
Whose eyes like twinkling stars in evening clear,
Were deck't with smyles, that all sad humours chased,
And darted forth delights, the which her goodly graced.
SPENSER.

Cheerful looks make every dish a feast,
And 't is that crowns a welcome.
MASSINGER.

What then remains but well our power to use,
And keep good humour still, whate'er we lose?
And trust me, dear, good humour can prevail,
When airs, and flights, and screams, and scolding fail;
Beauties in vain their pretty eyes may roll;
Charms strike the sight, but merit wins the soul.
POPE.

LEMATIS. *Clematis Virginiana.* Class 13, POLYANDRIA. Order : HEPTAGYNIA. This is a climbing shrub of rapid growth, ornamental, and highly fragrant. Its leaves are used by mendicants to produce ulcers, in order to excite commiseration. This infamousartifice is often the cause of real and permanent wounds. This genus embraces no less than thirty species which are distributed over all quarters of the globe. By some writers it is made the emblem of mental beauty ; by others, of artifice.

ARTIFICE.

Shallow artifice begets suspicion,
And like a cobweb veil but thinly shades
The face of thy design : alone disguising
What should have ne'er been seen ; imperfect mischief!
Thou, like the adder, venomous and deaf,
Hast stung the traveller ; and, after, hear'st
Not his pursuing voice ; e'en when thou think'st
To hide, the rustling leaves and bended grass
Confess and point the path which thou hast crept.
O fate of fools ! officious in contriving ;
In executing, puzzled, lame, and lost.
                                        CONGREVE.

What's the bent brow, or neck in thought reclined !
The body's wisdom to conceal the mind.
A man of sense can artifice disdain,
As men of wealth may venture to go plain ;
And be this truth eternal ne'er forgot,
Solemnity's a cover for a sot.
I find the fool when I behold the screen ;
For 't is the wise man's interest to be seen.
                                        YOUNG.

LEMATIS, ENGLISH. *Clematis Vitalba.* Class 13, Polyandria. Order: Pentagynia. This is called Traveller's Joy! "I do not know," says Miss Twamley, "its origin further than that the beauty of the plant is cheering to far travellers, clothing as it does the wayside hedges and banks." It is, however, a sweet, kindly old-fashioned name.

TRAVELLER'S JOY.

Who gave to thee that name,
So full of homely and most pleasant thought?
Its charm might win renown
For many a thing with far less beauty fraught.

There's something in it tells
Of wanderings ended brightly;—of the close,
'Mid old familiar scenes,
Of the tired wayfarer's amount of woes.

Wert thou the humblest flower
That we e'er scorn with that rude term, "a weed,
Thy *name* would unto me
For kindly thought and pleasant fancies plead.

But thou art beautiful,
And our sole native of thy graceful band,
Which we so prize, and seek,
In varied form and hue, through many a land.

How often have I paused,
A joyous traveller, in sooth, to cull
A garland of thy flowers,
When with faint sweets the sun had fill'd them full.

Twamley.

OLTSFOOT. *Tussilago Farfarus.* Class 19, SYNGENESIA. Order: SUPERFLUA. The odd name *Coltsfoot* was given from the fancied resemblance of the leaves to a colt's foot, and from the same cause it has been called, Horse-hoof, Foal-foot, and Bull-foot. The Latin name *Tussilago Farfarus* is from *tussis*, a cough, from its supposed efficacy in curing such complaints, and *farfarus*, a Greek term for the White Poplar, the leaves of which it resembles. Tinder is made from the cottony down on the under surface of its leaves, and they are sometimes smoked instead of tobacco.

MATERNAL CARE.

On scaly stem, with cottony down,
O'erlaid, its lemon-colour'd crown,
Which droop'd unclosed, but now erect,
The Colts-foot bright developes ; deck'd
(Ere yet the impurpled stalk displays
Its dark green leaves) with countless rays,
Round countless tubes, alike in dye,
Expanded.   MANT.

Belinda ! The young blossom that doth lie
So lightly on thy bosom, — clasp it there;
For on her brow an empress doth not wear,
Nor in her jewell'd zone, a gem more fair,
Or that doth deck her more becomingly.
Forget not then, that deep within thy flower
The germs lie hid of lovelier, holier things : —
Filial affection, that spontaneous springs;
High *truth* and maiden *purity ;* — the *power*
That comes of *gentleness ;* — ay, and more, —
Piety, nourish'd in the bosom's core ;
These, if so cherish'd, shall thy blossom bear,
And with the dews of heavenly love impearl'd,
It shall adorn thee in another world.
            WELLS.

OLUMBINE. *Aquilegia.* Class 13, POLY-
ANDRIA. Order : MONOGYNIA. This graceful flower has long been a favourite inhabit-
ant of the rustic flower border, and is commonly found in the open places of forests. or
extensive woods. It has been made the emblem of folly ;—why, it is difficult to say.

FOLLY.

Bring Lilies for a maiden's grave,
  Roses to deck the bride,
Tulips for all who love thro' life
  In brave attire to ride :
Bring each for each, in bower and hall,
But cull the Columbine for all.

"The Columbine? full many a flower
  Hath hues more clear and bright,
Although she doth in purple go,
  In crimson, pink, and white.
Why, when so many fairer shine,
Why choose the homely Columbine?"

"Know ye the cap which Folly wears
  In ancient masques and plays?
Does not the Columbine recal
  That toy of olden days?
And is not Folly reigning now
O'er many a wisdom-written brow?

"'Tis Folly's flower, that homely one;
  That universal guest
Makes every garden but a type
  Of every human breast;
For though ye tend both mind and bower,
There's still a nook for Folly's flower."

                                      TWAMLEY

ONVOLVULUS, or SEA BINDWEED. *Calystegia Soldanella.* Class 5, PENTANDRIA. Order: MONOGYNIA. Botanists have recently separated this flower from the genus Convolvulus, and name it *Calystegia*, from two Greek words signifying *pretty*, and *a covering*, the calyx of the flower being covered by two leaf-like appendages called bracts.

UNCERTAINTY.

On the low sandy shore,
Where, with a mighty roar,
Breakers, with foam-crest hoar,
    Long years have roll'd ;—
Where the turf never springs,
Where the wind's buffetings
Tear the poor flower, that clings
    To the rock cold.

There, Lady, low and lone,
Where, on the storm-blast's moan,
Comes the wreck'd sailor's groan,
    Is my chill dwelling ; —
I hear the signal gun,
Ere the storm's work is done;
I know that help is none,
I know the good ship's gone,
I know the tempest's won
    The triumph 't is telling.
TWAMLEY

Hope and fear alternate sway'd his breast,
Like light and shade upon a waving field,
Coursing each other, when the flying clouds
Now hide, and now reveal the sun.
HOME.

ONVOLVULUS. WHITE BINDWEED. *Calystegia Sepium.* Class 5, PENTANDRIA. Order : MONOGYNIA. This perennial twiner is a species of convolvulus, and is a very troublesome plant in the cornfield, where it is very commonly found. It is a simple flower; and probably on account of this quality it has been made the emblem of humility.

HUMILITY.

Lady, I dwell in the shady wood,
　Beneath the ancient trees;
And I hang o'er gnarled bole and branch
　My dainty tapestries.

I lie on my couch of arrowy leaves,
　And slumber with closed eye,
And only look out from my curtain'd bower,
　When the sun is rising high.

O'er bank and hedge, like a fairy camp,
　Gleam tent-like flowers of mine;
And elvish folk lie basking there,
　All through the noontide shine.

I love the river's sedgy bank,
　Where purple loose-strife bends,
Near fleur-de-lis, and meadow-sweet,
　All those dear ancient friends.

I love to twine around them all,
　And with fond arms to cling
Around the cluster'd stems and flowers
　In many a mazy ring.

　　　　　　　　　　　　TWAMLEY.

ONVOLVULUS, FIELD. Class 5, PENT-ANDRIA. Order: MONOGYNIA. This small pink flower rejoices in as many titles as any royal prince, for it is so common and so troublesome, as to have made itself a name in all rural vocabularies; among others, it is known as Weed-bind, Rope-weed, Bell-bind, Bell-wind, With-wind, and Hedgebells.

CAPTIVATION.

Come from the dim woods, come from the sea,
Come to the meadows and laugh with me;
Great heavy trees are gloomy things,
And dismally ever old Neptune sings;
 Come to the meadows bright,
 Where, in the sunny light,
 Over the blades of grass
 Soft-winged zephyrs pass;
  Come with me there.
 Come to the uplands high,
 Where the rich cornfields lie
  Golden and rare.
 Come from the shady woods,
 Come from the roaring floods,
Come, where the meadows lie fragrant and fair!
     TWAMLEY.

We merry flowers are running
 The meadow mazes through;
And be the farmers e'er so cunning,
 We're as cunning too!
And many a time the Farmer vows
 He'll banish us his land;
And we still run up the Hawthorn bough,
 A merry and myriad band.
     TWAMLEY.

RANBERRY. *Oxycoccus.* Class 8, OCTAN-
DRIA. Order: MONOGYNIA. This useful
berry is very abundant in the United States.
It commonly grows in and about the little
pools of the swampy moorlands, and the ga-
therers are often obliged to wade into the
water to come at them, so that the pittance
they thus win is dearly earned. The botanical name is one of
odd sound but good meaning, being *oxycoccus*, from two Greek
words meaning *acid* and *fruit*.

HARDINESS.

The Cranberry blossom dwelleth there
   Amid the mountains cold,
Seeming like a fairy gift
   Left on the dreary wold.

Oh! and 't is very beautiful,
   The flowers are pink and white,
And the small oval polish'd leaves
   Are evergreen and bright.

'T is such a wee, fair, dainty thing,
   You 'd think a greenhouse warm
Would be its proper dwelling place,
   Kept close from wind and storm.

But on the moors it dwelleth free
   Like a fearless mountain child;
With a rosy cheek, a lightsome look,
   And a spirit strong and wild.

The bushes all in water grow,
   In those small pools that lie
In scores among the turfy knolls
   On mountains broad and high.
                  TWAMLEY.

ROCUS. *Crocus.* Class 3, TRIANDRIA. Order: MONOGYNIA. According to the Grecian mythology, the name of this flower is derived from *Crocus,* a youth who was consumed by the ardour of his love for the nymph *Smilax,* and afterwards changed into the flower which bears his name. The common saffron used in medicine is a species of crocus, the *crocus sativus,* a native of Greece and Asia Minor.

CHEERFULNESS.

Oh ! many a glorious flower there grows
   In far and richer lands ;
But high in my affection e'er
   The Autumnal Crocus stands.

I love their faces, when by one
   And two they 're looking out :
I love them when the spreading field
   Is purple all about.

I loved them in the by-gone years
   Of childhood's thoughtless laughter,
When I marvell'd why the flowers came first,
   And the leaves the season after.

I loved them then, I love them now —
   The gentle and the bright ;
I love them for the thoughts they bring
   Of Spring's returning light ;

When, first-born of the waking earth,
   Their kindred gay appear,
And, with the Snow-drop, usher in
   The hope-invested year.

               HOWITT.

ROSS OF JERUSALEM. *Lychnis Visca-ria.* Class 16, DECANDRIA. Order: PEN-TAGYNIA. This flower, has been frequently named Cross of Jerusalem, in most of the European languages, the French calling it *croix de Jérusalem;* the Spanish, *cruces de Jerusalem;* the Italians, *croce di Cavalieri;* the Germans, *Hierosolymorum flos;* the Portuguese, *cruz de Malta;* all tending to dedicate it to religion, and as it appears to have been introduced by the crusaders, we present it as the emblem of religious enthusiasm.

DEVOTION

The maid who kept
In her young heart the secret of his love,
With all its hoarded store of sympathies
And images of hope, think ye she gave,
When a few years their fleeting course had run,
Her heart again to man?

No! no! She twined
Its riven tendrils round a surer prop,
And rear'd its blighted blossoms towards that sky
Which hath no cloud. She sought devotion's balm,
And, with a gentle sadness, turn'd her soul
From gaiety and song. Pleasure, for her,
Had lost its essence, and the viol's voice
Gave but a sorrowing sound. Even her loved plants
Breathed too distinctly of the form that bent
With hers to watch their budding. 'Mid their flowers,
And through the twining of their puerile stems,
The semblance of a cold, dead hand would rise,
Until she bade them droop and pass away
With him she mourn'd.

SIGOURNEY.

ROWN IMPERIAL. *Fritillaria Imperialis.* Class 6, HEXANDRIA. Order: MONO-GYNIA. This noble flower is said to have been brought into England in the time of Shakspeare, who has introduced it in his Winter's Tale:

> Bold oxlip, and
> The crown imperial; lilies of all kinds;
> The flower de luce being one.

On this family of plants modern botanists have bestowed the name of Fritillaria, of which this, from its commanding deport-ment and brilliant colours, is considered the sovereign.

> The lily's height bespoke command,
>   A fair imperial flower;
> She seem'd design'd for Flora's hand,
>   The sceptre of her power.

We have therefore elevated this distinguished member of Flora's kingdom to be the emblem of majesty, and the representative of power in our floral sentiments.

MAJESTY.

> There *is* for Kings a fame that never dies,
> A sunlike glory which itself supplies,
> The light that emanates from grateful minds,
> Defying envy, which its lustre blinds.
> There is, for ever flowing and to flow,
> For Him who turns to joy his people's woe,
> A stream of love unwearied in its course,
> A nation's heart its warm and salient source.
> Through loyal veins, devolved from sires to sons,
> From age to age the faithful current runs,
> And bears for ever on in just renown
> The buoyant name that dignified a crown.
> One Patriot King has earn'd this meed of fame,
> And Ireland's voice will vindicate His claim.

QUILLINAN.

YCLAMEN. *Cyclamen.* Class 5, PENTAN-DRIA. Order: MONOGYNIA. As modest dif-fidence adds attractions to beauty, so does this graceful flower engage our notice by its unassuming carriage, for the cyclamen, al-though it expands its petals in an upright direction, never rears its head to the sun.

We present this emblem with a hope that the poets will not longer remain too diffident to let this pretty plant escape the har-mony of their song, since we cannot find a line to form a motto, or grace the floral symbol of diffidence.

"Distress makes the humble heart diffident."

The church has dedicated this flower to St. Romuald.

DIFFIDENCE.

The modest virtues mingled in her eyes,
Still on the ground dejected, darting all
Their humid beams into the blooming flowers.
THOMSON.

As lamps burn silent, with unconscious light,
So modest ease in beauty shines most bright;
Unaiming charms with edge resistless fall,
And she who means no mischief, does it all.
HILL.

I pity bashful men, who feel the pain
Of fancied scorn and undeserved disdain,
And bear the marks upon a blushing face
Of needless shame, and self-imposed disgrace.
Our sensibilities are so acute,
The fear of being silent makes us mute.
COWPER.

He saw her charming, but he saw not half
The charms her downcast modesty conceal'd.
THOMSON.

YPRESS. *Cupressus Sempervirens.* Class 2, MONŒCIA. Order: MONADELPHIA. The cypress is the universal emblem of mourning, and is the funeral tree in the eastern world, from the Persian Gulf to the Caspian Sea; it is also dedicated to the dead, from Mazanderan to Constantinople, as well as to the utmost bounds of China's fruitful shores.

Ovid gives us a traditionary account of the mournful origin of the cypress tree, and we always find it devoted to mournful thoughts, or sad solemnities. Cyparissus, son of Telephus of Cea, was beloved by Apollo. Having killed the favourite stag of his friend, he grieved, pined, and, dying, was changed by Apollo into a cypress tree. Calmet describes it to be a tall, straight tree, having bitter leaves. The shade and smell were said to be dangerous; hence the Romans looked on it as a fatal tree, and made use of it at funerals. It is an evergreen; the wood is heavy, of rather a fragrant smell,—is not liable to be attacked by insects, and does not speedily decay. Shakspeare says that cypress is the emblem of mourning; and we are told by Irving that, in Latium, on the decease of any person, a branch of cypress was placed before the door.

MOURNING.

A funeral train
Will in a cypress grove be found.

LANDON.

The moon is o'er a grove of cypress trees
Weeping like mourners.

LANDON.

Peace to the dust that in silence reposes
    Beneath the dark shades of cypress and yew;
Let spring deck the spot with her earliest roses,
    And heaven wash their leaves with its holiest dew.

PIERPONT.

AFFODIL. *Narcissus Major.* Class 6, HEXANDRIA. Order: MONOGYNIA. This is a Spanish plant. It is the largest of the genus, and has splendid flowers. It is generally found double in gardens, rarely single. The Daffodil, says the Flora Historica, was evidently considered a kind of lily by early writers, and we are of opinion that the name is a corruption of *Dis's Lily,* as it is the flower supposed to be dropped from the chariot of that god, in his flight with *Proserpine.*

CHIVALRY.

>   'T is much he dares;
> And to that dauntless temper of his mind,
> He hath a wisdom that doth guide his valour
> To act in safety.
>
> SHAKSPEARE.

> He is a man, setting his fate aside,
> Of comely virtues:
> Nor did he soil the fact with cowardice
> (An honour in him, which buys out his fault);
> But, with a noble fury, and fair spirit,
> Seeing his reputation touch'd to death,
> He did oppose his foe:
> And with such sober and unnoted passion
> He did behave his anger, ere 't was spent,
> As if he had but proved an argument.
>
> SHAKSPEARE.

>   The dearest friend, the kindest man,
> The best condition'd and unwearied spirit
> In doing courtesies.
>
> SHAKSPEARE.

AHLIA. *Dahlia.* Class 19, SYNGENESIA. Order: POLYGAMIA SUPERFLUA. Named in honour of Andrew Dahl, a Swedish botanist. A mountain flower of South America, recently become very fashionable among the florists of the United States, who vie with each other in the number and beauty of the different varieties which they cultivate, and which form the chief ornament of all our horticultural exhibitions.

FOR EVER THINE.

Yes! still I love thee:—Time, who sets
  His signet on my brow;
And dims my sunken eye, forgets
  The heart he could not bow;
Where love, that cannot perish, grows
For one, alas! that little knows
  How love may sometimes last;
  Like sunshine wasting in the skies,
  When clouds are overcast.

The dew-drop hanging o'er the rose,
  Within its robe of light,
Can never touch a leaf that blows,
  Though seeming to the sight;
And yet it still will linger there,
Like hopeless love without despair,—
  A snow-drop in the sun!
  A moment finely exquisite,
  Alas! but only one.
                              DAWES.

AISY. *Bellis.* Class 19, Syngenesia. Order: Polygamia Superflua. Fabulous history informs us that the Daisy owed its origin to Belides, one of the nymphs called Dryads, who were supposed to preside over meadows and pastures. While dancing on the turf with Ephigeus, whose suit she encouraged, she attracted the admiration of Vertumnus, the deity who presided over orchards; and to escape from him, she was transformed into the humble flower, the Latin name of which is Bellis. The ancient English name of this flower was Day's Eye, in which way it is written by Ben Jonson; and Chaucer calls it the "ee of the daie." No doubt it received this designation from its habit of closing its petals at night, which it also does in rainy weather.

INNOCENCE.

When, smitten by the morning ray,
I see thee rise, alert and gay,
Then, cheerful flower! my spirits play
    With kindred gladness:

And when, at dark, by dews opprest,
Thou sink'st, the image of thy rest
Hath often eased my pensive breast
    Of careful sadness.

Wordsworth.

Heav'n may awhile correct the virtuous,
Yet it will wipe their eyes again, and make
Their faces whiter with their tears. Innocence
Conceal'd is the stol'n pleasure of the gods,
Which never ends in shame, as that of men
Doth oftentimes do; but like the sun breaks forth,
When it hath gratified another world;
And to our unexpecting eyes appears
More glorious thro' its late obscurity.

Fountain.

ANDELION. *Leontodon Taraxacum.* Class 19, SYNGENESIA. Order: POLYGAMIA ÆQUALIS. Linnæus has given the dandelion a deserved place in the horologe of Flora. It is one of the plants that may be most certainly depended upon as to the hour of opening and closing its flowers. The flower, if we well examine it, we shall discover to be fully as handsome as the fine garden anemone; and it only needs to be as rare to be prized as much. This plant blossoms early in the spring, and continues through the summer.

ORACLE.

Thine full many a pleasing bloom
Of blossoms lost to all perfume;
Thine the dandelion flowers,
Gilt with dew like sun with showers.
                               CLARE.

Miss Landon wrote some very beautiful lines, on seeing an illustration of the garden scene in Goethe's Faust, where Margaret plucks a star-like flower to divine the real sentiments of her lover. They are called "The Decision of the Flower."

And with scarlet poppies around, like a bower,
The maiden found her mystic flower;
" Now, gentle flower, I pray thee tell
If my lover loves me, and loves me well;
So may the fall of the morning dew
Keep the sun from fading thy tender blue.

Now I number the leaves for my lot —
He loves not — he loves me — he loves me not —
He loves me, — yes, thou last leaf, yes —
I'll pluck thee not for that last sweet guess !
He loves me !"— " Yes," a dear voice sigh'd,
And her lover stands by Margaret's side.

OGWOOD. *Cornus Florida.* Class **4,** TETRANDRIA. Order: MONOGYNIA. The Dogwood is found in all parts of the United States, south of latitude 43 degrees, and is well known from the large white petaloid involucres, which render it so conspicuous in the spring. It does not usually exceed twenty feet in height, but the wood is hard, compact, and excellently adapted for the handles of light tools and similar purposes.

LOVE UNDIMINISHED BY ADVERSITY.

There's an hour when the heart, like a bark o'er the waves,
  Seems nearing the port so long anxiously sought,
And the tempests of passion lie hush'd in their caves,
  And life's gales from the soul a sweet odour have caught;
But the eye may deceive, and the wish may betray,
  And the port prove a cloud, or a desolate isle ;
And the heart and the cheek which were happy to-day,
  May to-morrow have lost both their hope and their smile.

Oh ! the love I would die for, or live but to prize,
  Is that which through seasons of sorrow hath pass'd ;
Like the radiant light of the midsummer skies,
  Shines on through our lives, but grows loveliest at last ;
The hearts which are form'd but in sunshine and flowers,
  Enraptured to beat, or united to cling,
Know not the bliss shed by Time's truth-testing powers,
  O'er those whose affections have blunted grief's sting.
                              THE KNICKERBOCKER.

                   Love does reign
In stoutest minds, and maketh monstrous war:
He maketh war, he maketh peace again,
And yet his peace is but continual jar:
O miserable men that to him subject are.
                              SPENSER.

 GLANTINE, or EUROPEAN SWEET BRIAR. *Rosa Rubiginosa.* Class 12, Ico-sandria. Order: Polygynia. The eglantine, or wild briar rose, more commonly called sweet briar, has ever been considered the poet's flower. It is not loved for its fair delicate blossoms only; but its fragrant leaves, which perfume the breeze of dewy morn, and the soft breath of eve, entitle it to its frequent association with the woodbine or honeysuckle.

POETRY.

Its sides I'll plant with dew-sweet eglantine,
And honeysuckles full of clear bee-wine.

KEATS.

Yonder is a girl who lingers
Where wild honeysuckle grows,
Mingled with the briar rose.

H. SMITH.

A sweeter spot on earth was never found:
I look'd, and look'd, and still with new delight;
Such joy my soul, such pleasures fill'd my sight;
And the fresh eglantine exhaled a breath,
Whose odours were of power to raise from death.

DRYDEN.

Boon nature scatter'd, free and wild,
Each plant or flower, the mountain's child,
Here eglantine embalm'd the air,
Hawthorn and hazel mingled there;
The primrose pale, and violet flower,
Found in each cliff a narrow bower.

SCOTT.

LM. *Ulmus.* Class 5, **Pentandria.** Order: **Digynia.** The elm is a very majestic tree; in beauty, dignity, and usefulness, yielding only to the oak. Gilpin gives preference to the ash in his scale of excellence, because it has more of individuality than the elm, which he esteems a great source of picturesque beauty. But his objection applies to the tree only in its skeleton state. When in full leaf, the elm shows itself an elm.

DIGNITY.

> Follow me, as I sing
> And touch the warbled string;
> Under the shady roof
> Of branching elm, star-proof,
> Follow me!

Anon.

> Ye fallen avenues! once more I mourn
> Your fate unmerited, once more rejoice
> That yet a remnant of your race survives.
> How airy and how light the graceful arch!
> Yet awful as the consecrated roof
> Re-echoing pious anthems! while beneath
> The checker'd earth seems restless as a flood
> Brush'd by the wind. So sportive is the light
> Shot through the boughs, it dances as they dance,
> Shadow and sunshine intermingling quick,
> And dark'ning and enlight'ning, as the leaves
> Play wanton, ev'ry moment, ev'ry spot.

Cowper.

> ———There, fast rooted in their bank,
> Stand, never overlook'd, our favourite elms.

Cowper.

NCHANTER'S NIGHTSHADE. *Cir-cæa*. Class 2, DIANDRIA. Order: MONO-GYNIA. The species Lutetiana is found in North America and Europe. As the name of this plant indicates, it is celebrated in magical incantations. Its flowers are rose-coloured, and veined with purple. It com-monly grows in damp and shady places, where shrubs fit for the purpose to which this has been applied may be supposed to be found. It is named Circæa after the enchantress Circe.

FASCINATION.

The night-shade strews to work him ill.
DRAYTON.

———————— O, who can tell
The hidden power of herbes, and might of magic spell!
SPENSER.

'T is now the very witching time of night.
I 'll witch, sweet ladies, with my words and looks.
SHAKSPEARE.

For Circe had long loved the youth in vain,
Till love refused, converted to disdain:
Then mixing pow'rful herbs, with magic art,
She changed his form, who could not change his heart.
DRYDEN.

For he by words could call out of the sky
Both sun and moon, and make them him obey:
The land to sea, and sea to main-land dry,
And darksome night he eke could turn to day;
Huge hosts of men he could alone dismay,
And hosts of men of meanest things could frame,
Whenso him list his enemies to fray,
That to this day for terror of his fame
The fiends do quake, when any him to them does name,
SPENSER.

VENING PRIMROSE. *Œnothera.* Class 8, OCTANDRIA. Order: MONOGYNIA. It is uncertain when this beautiful flower was first introduced into England, though we know that it was brought from Virginia to Padua, in the year 1619. It is a general favourite with our poets, who give it a very different character to that we have assigned to it in floral language. We presume that it has been made the emblem of in-constancy on account of the transient duration of its flowers. It opens between six and seven o'clock in the evening.

INCONSTANCY

When once the sun sinks in the west,
And dew-drops pearl the Evening's breast;
Almost as pale as moon-beams are,
Or its companionable star,
The evening primrose opes anew
Its delicate blossoms to the dew;
And, hermit-like, shunning the light,
Wastes its fair bloom upon the Night,
Who, blindfold to its fond caresses,
Knows not the beauty he possesses.
Thus it blooms on while Night is by;
When Day looks out with open eye,
'Bash'd at the gaze it cannot shun,
It faints, and withers, and is gone.

CLARE.

How long must women wish in vain
  A constant love to find?
No art can fickle man retain,
  Or fix a roving mind.
Yet fondly we ourselves deceive,
  And empty hopes pursue;
Though false to others, we believe
  They will to us prove true.

SHADWELL.

VERGREEN THORN. *Mespilus Pyracantha.* Class 12, Icosandria. Order: Digynia. This well-known shrub is a native of the south of Europe: it also grows plentifully on Mount Caucasus, in the Chersonesus, and in China. It was introduced into England early in the seventeenth century, but has never yet got beyond the pale of the garden or shrubbery, notwithstanding Evelyn's hint that it might be cultivated, with little trouble, for fences and other common purposes.

SOLACE IN ADVERSITY.

Thou wast not born when merry May
" Hangs out the virgin flag of spring,"
When birds from every bush and spray
    Are carolling.

Thou wast not born when summer throws
Her glory over sky and earth,
Nor did the beam which wakes the rose
    Smile on thy birth.

No; like this shrub which cheers the bower,
What time the threatening storm is rife,
A blessing for the wintry hour
    Thou sprang to life.

And such art still—no summer friend,
Breathing smooth things in Pleasure's ear;
But, oh! let grief the spirit rend,
    And thou art near.

What could I less than love the hour
Which stills the bird, and strips the lea,
Since, oh! to cheer the social bower,
    It gave us thee.
        Anon.

ENNEL. *Anethum.* Class 5, PENTANDRIA. Order: DIGYNIA. The gladiators mingled this plant with their food, from a supposition that it tended to increase their strength. After the games were over, the conqueror was crowned with a wreath of fennel. The Romans named the plant anethum.

STRENGTH.

One fire drives out another; one nail, one nail;
Rights by rights founder, strengths by strengths do fail.

SHAKSPEARE.

Hercules himself must yield to odds;
And many strokes, though with a battle-axe,
Hew down and fell the hardest timber'd oak.

SHAKSPEARE.

Blood hath bought blood, and blows have answer'd blows;
Strength match'd with strength, and power confronted power.

SHAKSPEARE.

All the soul
Of man is resolution; which expires
Never from valiant men, till their last breath;
And then with it, like a flame extinguish'd
For want of matter; it does not die, but
Rather ceases to live.

CHAPMAN.

If your resolutions be like mine,
We will yet give our sorrows a brave end.
Justice is for us, so may fortune be:
I'm a bright proof of her inconstancy.
But if no god will lend us any aid,
Let us be gods, and fortune to ourselves.

CROWN.

ERN. *Filicia.* Class 24, CRYPTOGAMIA. Order: FIRST OF THIS CLASS. Fern often affords an agreeable seat to lovers; its ashes are used in the manufacture of glasses for the convivial party; and all the world knows that love and wine make men sincere.

SINCERITY.

The green and graceful Fern,
  How beautiful it is!
There's not a leaf in all the land
  So wonderful, I wis.

Have ye ever watch'd it budding,
  With each stem and leaf wrapp'd small,
Coiled up within each other
  Like a round and hairy ball?

Have ye watch'd that ball unfolding
  Each closely nestling curl,
And its fair and feathery leaflets
  Their spreading forms unfurl?

Oh! then most gracefully they wave
  In the forest, like a sea,
And dear as they are beautiful
  Are these *Fern* leaves to me.

For all of early childhood—
  Those past and blessed years
To which we ever wistfully
  Look back through memory's tears—

The sports and fancies then my own,
  Those *Fern* leaves dear and wild
Bring back to my delighted breast—
  I am once more a child.

                              TWAMLEY.

FLAX. *Linum.* Class 5, PENTANDRIA. Order: PENTAGYNIA. Truly we ought to be grateful to this useful plant! It yields us the linen we wear, the paper we write upon, and the lace which adorns our fair countrywomen. Nowhere can we cast our eyes but we see evidence of its utility. It has been cultivated from time inmemorial for the lint and tow it affords, and it was formerly the chief occupation of cottagers' wives to spin this into yarn and linen cloth.

I FEEL YOUR KINDNESS.

Ah! 'tis a goodly little thing,
  It groweth for the poor,
And many a peasant blesses it,
  Beside his cottage door.
He thinketh how those slender stems
  That shimmer in the sun,
Are rich for him in web and woof,
  And shortly shall be spun.
He thinketh how those tender flowers
  Of seed will yield him store;
And sees in thought his next year's crop,
  Blue, shining round his door.

Oh! the goodly Flax-flower!
  It groweth on the hill;
And be the breeze awake or sleep,
  It never standeth still!
It seemeth all astir with life,
  As if it loved to thrive,
As if it had a merry heart
  Within its stem alive!
Then fair befal the Flax-field;
  And may the kindly showers
Give strength unto its shining stems,
  Give seed unto its flowers.

MARY HOWITT.

OXGLOVE. *Digitalis.* Class 14, DIDY-NAMIA. Order: ANGIOSPERMIA. Where is the Garden-guest that may outshine the stately, tall, magnificent Foxglove? This is as remarkable for its majestic, lofty demeanour, as the light, lithe Harebell for its modest playfulness. The tall spiral stem, springing up from the group of broad leaves, and thickly hung with the beautiful purple blossoms, gradually lessening in size from the large open bells on the lower portion of the stalk, to the little bud on the summit, still wrapped up in their close green calices, is an object so strikingly beautiful, that I should think any person who had once given it an attentive observance must inevitably be a lover of flowers to the end of his days.

STATELINESS.

The Foxgloves and the Fern,
    How gracefully they grow
Vith grand old oaks above them
    And wavy grass below !
'The stately trees stand round
    Like columns fair and high,
And the spreading branches bear
    A glorious canopy
Of leaves, that rustling wave
    In the whispering summer air,
And gaily greet the sunbeams
    That are falling brightly there.
The miser-leaves ! — they suffer
    Not a gleam to twinkle through,
And in the Foxglove's hairy cup,
    At noonday, drops of dew
Are hanging round like tears
    Of sorrow, that the sun
Gives to other flowers his kisses,
    But to her soft lips not one.
                          TWAMLEY.

UCHSIA, GLOBEFLOWERED. *Fuchsia Globosa.* Class 8, OCTANDRIA. Order: MONOGYNIA. This is a plant of great beauty, perhaps, says Paxton, exceeding any other species or variety of the Fuchsia known. It is dwarf and somewhat spreading, and the slender branches are somewhat sparingly covered with leaves, which are not of a large size.

CONFIDING LOVE.

Bless the hour Endearment gives!
Who on earth's cold climate lives,
But has felt his heart rejoice,
When woman's smile, and woman's voice,
Hath sent, with magical control,
All sweetness to the soften'd soul?

Oh! Happiness, where art thou found
(If indeed on mortal ground)
But with faithful hearts alone,
That Love and Friendship have made one —
In tenderness and faith sincere,
In affection's sweetest tear.

It was a livelong holiday;
　　And in that boat, far from the faithless crowd,
　　They who true love and mutual trust avow'd,
Pursued in peace their solitary way.
And it was bliss to see the manly youth,
Whose look bespoke sincerity and truth,
Gaze upon her he loved, as he could bless
Th' Almighty Being, in the living light
Of whose warm sun he felt such happiness,
Whilst tears of transport almost dimm'd his sight.

BOWLES.

ERANIUM. *Pelargonium.* Class 16, Mo-
NADELPHIA. Order : HEPTANDRIA. Among
the gayest of the floral court are the richly
clad Geraniums. Fashion and culture have
contributed so much to the aggrandizement
of the beautiful tribe of Pelargoniums, or,
as they are generally, but erroneously call-
ed Geraniums, that they now count a greater number of royal
and illustrious titles in their family than any other species of
flower can boast.

GENTILITY

I said the Lily was the queenly flower,
 And these bright creatures, sure, her courtiers be !
 For they are robed all so royally,
E'en like the glittering guests of regal bower;
And, like them too, their chiefest rank and power
 Lie in their sounding titles, and we see
 That both do value the embroiderie
Of their gay-tinted garb. In their first hour
Of modish fame, see how to both down bend,
 In fashion's homage, all the wondering crowd
Of sycophant adorers ! Should chance send
 A newer star, how soon into a cloud
Shrink the late idols! whom no more ye find ;
Nor have they either left ye any sweet behind.
TWAMLEY.

  Athenia is a noble gentlewoman,
Stamp'd in the finest mould of excellence.
Rome in her palmiest state, when woman nursed
Her grandeur, by the care of her young heroes,
Had scarce her equal.
DAWES.

ILLYFLOWER.   *Cheiranthus Incanus.* Class 15, TETRADYNAMIA.   Order: SILI- QUOSA.   The gillyflower,—less graceful than the rose,—less superb than the lily,— has a splendour more durable.   Constant in its benefits, it offers to us, all the year, its beautiful red and pyramidal flowers, which always diffuse an agreeable odour.   The finest gillyflowers are red ; they derive their name from their colour, which rivals in brilliancy the far-famed purple of Tyre.   White, violet, and variegated gillyflowers have also their charms.   This beautiful flower may be said to grow in our parterres, like a blooming and lively beauty, who scatters health around her ; health, that chief of blessings, without which there can be neither happiness nor lasting beauty.

LASTING BEAUTY.

'Tis not alone in the flush of morn,
In the cowslip-bell or the blossom thorn,
In noon's high hour, or twilight's hush,
In the shadowy stream, or the rose's blush,
Or in aught that bountiful Nature gives,
That the delicate Spirit of Beauty lives.

Oh no ! it lives and breathes, and lies,
In a home more pure than the morning skies ;
In the innocent heart it loves to dwell,
When it comes with a sigh or a tear to tell
Sweet visions that flow from a fount of love,
To mingle with all that is pure above.

Sweet Spirit of Beauty ! my dreams are thine,
But I lose thee not when thy day-beams shine ;
Thy image is still to my constant gaze,
At midnight hour or noontide blaze ;
And none but one with a heart unsold,
Can know the bliss which thy lovers hold.

DAWES.

LORY FLOWER, CRIMSON. *Clianthus Puniceus.* Class 17, DIADELPHIA. Order: DECANDRIA. This new and beautiful shrub is a native of New Zealand, whence seeds of it were sent to England by the Missionaries in that part. The native name is Kowaingutu Kaha, or Parrot-bill, most probably called so from the resemblance to the bill of a bird.

GLORIOUS BEAUTY.

The Spirit of Beauty unfurls her light,
And wheels her course in a joyous flight;
I know her track through the balmy air,
By the blossoms that cluster and whiten there;
She leaves the tops of the mountains green,
And gems the valley with crystal sheen.

At morn, I know where she rested at night,
For the roses are gushing with dewy delight;
Then she mounts again, and round her flings
A shower of light from her crimson wings;
Till the spirit is drunk with the music on high,
That silently fills it with ecstasy.

At noon she hies to a cool retreat;
Where bowering elms over waters meet,
She dimples the wave where the green leaves dip,
As it smilingly curls like a maiden's lip,
When her tremulous bosom would hide, in vain,
From her lover, the hope that she loves again.

She hovers around us at twilight hour,
When her presence is felt with the deepest power,
She silvers the landscape, and crowds the stream
With shadows that flit like a fairy dream;
Then wheeling her flight through the gladden'd air,
The Spirit of Beauty is everywhere.

DAWES.

ORSE. *Ulex Europæus.* Class **17,** Diadelphia. Order: Decandria. The botanical name *Ulex* is obscure; we call it in-
discriminately Furze, Gorse or Whin. The
common wild Gorse of England, in St. Pe-
tersburg is cherished in the choicest green-
houses, and esteemed one of their most
precious ornaments, as it flowers in winter. In England the
commons are covered in the richest profusion with its gay, beautiful, and fragrant flowers.

CHEERFULNESS IN ADVERSITY.

Fair maidens, I'll sing you a song;
   I'll tell you the bonny wild flower,
Whose blossoms so yellow, and branches so long,
O'er moor and o'er rough rocky mountain are flung,
   Far away from trim garden and bower.

It clings to the crag, and it clothes the wild hill;
   It stands sturdily breasting the storm,
When the loud-voiced winds sing so drearily shrill,
And the snow-flakes in eddies fall silent and still,
   And the shepherd can scarce wrap him warm.

'T is the bonny bright Gorse, that gleams cheerily forth,
   Like sunlight e'er lingering here,
In the verdure of Spring, and when Summer on earth
Has call'd all the fairest of blossoms to birth,
   As a crown for the noon of the year.

Twamley.

And her against sweet cheerfulness was placed,
Whose eyes, like twinkling stars in evening clear,
Were deck'd with smiles, that all sad humours chased,
And darted forth delights, the which her goodly graced.

Spenser.

RASS. *Gramen.* Class 3, TRIANDRIA. Order: DIGYNIA. It will be admitted that what is the most useful, is in nature the most common; and of all vegetable productions, what is there more common than grass? It clothes the earth with a verdant carpet, and it yields food,—nay, it "grows for the cattle," in obedience to the Creator's word.

UTILITY.

'Tis pleasant, on the steep hill-side,
Where lies in view the prospect wide
Of cultured farm, with interchange
Of tilth and pasture, cot and grange,
At ease the careless limbs to stretch
Beneath the broad o'er-arching beech,
And, lighted by the sky serene,
Mark the full hay-field's varied scene.
Here, as the swarthy mowers pass
Slow through the tall and russet grass,
In marshalling rank from side to side,
With circling stroke and measured stride,
Before the scythe's wide-sweeping sway
The russet meadow's tall array
Falls, and the bristly surface strows
With the brown swathe's successive rows.
.   .   .   .
And then the toiling horses strain,
Slowly to move the ponderous wain.
From pile to pile the slow wain goes,
And still at each more lofty grows;
While the stout swains below supply
Fresh fardels to the swains on high,
Heaps upon heaps the grassy load:
Thence, lumbering o'er the homeward road,
It swells, adorn'd with trophied bough,
The rich compact, or treasured mow.   MANT.

AREBELL. *Hyacinthus non-scriptus.* Class 6, HEXANDRIA. Order: MONOGYNIA. This beautiful little flower is a native of Persia; but is found in most parts of Europe. Our woods in the Spring present a lively appearance, from the mixture of their azure blue bells among the pale yellow primroses, and the many different-tinted heaths, so tastefully intermingled by the hand of Nature. It is called Harebell from its generally growing in those places frequented by hares: the flower varies in colour and beauty; some being completely white, and others much resembling the poorer kinds of hyacinths; but they have longer and narrower flowers, not swelling at the bottom; the bunch of flowers is likewise longer and bends downwards. The fresh roots of this plant are said to be poisonous; the juice is mucilaginous, and in the time of Queen Elizabeth was used as starch.

SUBMISSION.

Sweet flower! though many a ruthless storm
Sweep fiercely o'er thy slender form,
And many a sturdier plant may bow
In death beneath the tempest's blow,
Submissive thou, in pensive guise,
Uninjured by each gale shalt rise,
And, deck'd with innocence, remain
The fairest tenant of the plain:
So, conscious of its lowly state,
Trembles the heart assail'd by fate;
Yet, when the fleeting blast is o'er,
Settles as tranquil as before;
While the proud breast no peace shall find,
No refuge for a troubled mind.

ANON.

AWTHORN. *Cratægus.* Class 12, Ico-SANDRIA. Order: DIGYNIA. The hawthorn has been made the emblem of hope because the young and beautiful Athenian maids brought its branches, covered with flowers, to decorate their companions on their nuptial day, whilst they bare larger boughs of it to the altar. The altar of Hymen was lighted by torches made from the wood of this tree; and it also formed the flambeaux which illuminated the nuptial chamber. We are told that the Troglodytes, in the simplicity of their minds, tied hawthorn branches to the dead bodies of their parents and friends; and at the interment of the corpse they strewed its branches upon the body, and afterwards covered it with stones, laughing through the whole of the ceremony. They considered death as the dawning of a life which should never cease.

HOPE.

Now *hawthorns* blossom, now the daisies spring.
POPE.

See now, to grace the coppice wild,
May-born, our Britain's native child,
The Medlar's broad and single eye;
And, prized for village pharmacy,
The Elder's crowded cups minute;
Service, with tupe of Autumn fruit;
And Maple's spikes of florets green;
And *Hawthorn*, famed 'mid vernal scene
For gracing May's propitious hour
With prodigality of flower,
Pink-anther'd 'mid its petals pale,
And lending fragrance to the gale;
Hail'd from its fair and sweet array
The namesake of the lovely May.
TWAMLEY.

AZEL. *Corylus Avellana.* Class 21, Mo-
NŒCIA. Order: POLYANDRIA. There was
a time when men were not united by any
common tie. When the mother would de-
prive her son of the wild fruit with which
he wished to appease his hunger, and if misfortune united them for a moment, the sud-
den sight of an oak laden with acorns, or a beech covered with
beech-mast, rendered them enemies.

According to ancient mythology the gods had pity on the human race. Apollo and Mercury exchanged presents, and came
down upon the earth. The god of harmony received from the
son of Maïa a tortoise shell, of which he had made a lyre, and
gave in return a branch of hazel, which had the power of making
virtue beloved, and of re-uniting hearts divided by hatred and
envy. Thus armed, the two sons of Jupiter presented themselves
to men. Apollo first sang that eternal wisdom which had created the universe; filial piety and patriotic love were brought
into action, by his eloquence, to unite the human race; and commerce he made the bond of the world. His last thought was the
most sublime, for it was consecrated to the gods; and he told
mankind that they might become equal with the gods by deeds
of love and beneficence.

Ornamented with two light wings, and serpents entwining themselves around it, the hazel wand, presented to the god of eloquence
by the god of harmony, is still, under the name of Mercury's
wand, the symbol of peace, commerce, and reconciliation.

RECONCILIATION.

> And see,
> As yet unclothed, the Hazel-tree
> Prepares his early tufts to lend
> The coppice first fruits; and depend
> In russet drops, whose cluster'd rows,
> Still closed in part, in part disclose,
> Yet fenced beneath their scaly shed,
> The pendent anther's yellow head.   MANT.

 EART'S EASE. *Viola Tricolor.* Class 5, PENTANDRIA. Order: MONOGYNIA. The tints of this flower are scarce less varied than the names that have been bestowed upon it. That of pansy is a corruption of the French name, *pensée,* thought.

Leigh Hunt introduces the heart's-ease into his verses:

> The garden's gem,
> Heart's-ease, like a gallant bold,
> In his cloth of purple and gold.

Phillips observes that the most brilliant purples of the artist appear dull when compared to that of the pansy; our richest satins and velvets coarse and unsightly by a comparison of texture; and as to delicacy of shading, it is scarcely surpassed by the bow of Iris itself.

THINK OF ME.

> Frolick virgins once these were,
> Overloving, living here ;
> Being here their ends denied,
> Ran for sweethearts mad, and died.
>
> Love, in pitie of their teares,
> And their losse in blooming yeares,
> For their restlesse here-spent houres,
> Gave them heart's-ease turn'd to flowres.
>
> HERRICK.

> ———— And there are pansies, that's for thoughts.
> SHAKSPEARE.

> And thou, so rich in gentle names, appealing
>   To hearts that own our nature's common lot ;
> Those, styled by sportive fancy's better feeling
>   'A Thought,' 'The Heart's Ease,' or 'Forget me not.'
> BARTON.

EATH. *Erica.* Class 8, OCTANDRIA. Order: MONOGYNIA. The foliage of this plant is ever-green, of varied and beautiful shapes, and on examination is found as pleasing as its singular blossom. In our floral hieroglyphics it is made emblematical of solitude; and thus, when the rustic lover offers his mistress a bouquet of heath and pansies, she understands that if his solitude were charmed by her society his heart would be at ease.

SOLITUDE.

> The Erica here
> That o'er the Caledonian hills sublime
> Spreads its dark mantle (where the bees delight
> To seek their purest honey), flourishes;
> Sometimes with bells like amethysts, and then,
> Paler, and shaded like the maiden's cheek
> With gradual blushes—other while, as white
> As rime that hangs upon the frozen spray.
> Of this, old Scotia's hardy mountaineers
> Their rustic couches form; and there enjoy
> Sleep, which, beneath his velvet canopy,
> Luxurious idleness implores in vain.
>
> TWAMLEY.

> Oh! to lie down in wilds apart,
>   Where man is seldom seen or heard,
> In still and ancient forests, where
> Mows not his scythe, ploughs not his share,
>   With the shy deer and cooing bird!

> To go, in dreariness of mood,
>   O'er a lone heath, that spreads around
> A solitude like a silent sea,
> Where rises not a hut or tree,
>   The wide-embracing sky its bound!
>
> HOWITT

ELIOTROPE. *Heliotropium.* Class 5, PENTANDRIA. Order: MONOGYNIA. There are more than thirty species of this delicate and sweet-scented flower. The most valued by American florists are *Peruvianum*, *Corymbosum*, and *Grandiflorum*. The former is a universal favourite.

INTOXICATED WITH PLEASURE.

Methinks I've cast full twenty years aside,
And am again a boy. Every breath
Of air that trembles through the window bears
Unusual odour.

PROCTOR.

What's i' the air? —
Some subtle spirit runs thro' all my veins.
Hope seems to ride this morning on the wind,
And joy outshines the sun.

PROCTOR.

O sages! think on joy like this,
And where's your boast of apathy.

MOORE.

Each sound too here to languishment inclined,
Lull'd the weak bosom, and induced ease,
Aerial music in the warbling wind,
At distance rising oft, by small degrees,
Nearer and nearer came, till o'er the trees
It hung, and breathed such soul-dissolving airs,
As did, alas! with soft perdition please:
Entangled deep in its enchanting snares,
The list'ning heart forgot all duties and all cares.

THOMSON.

ICKORY. *Carya alba.* Class 21, MONŒ-CIA. Order: POLYANDRIA. The Hickory is found in most parts of the United States, and also produces nuts of excellent quality, which are everywhere well known. The wood of the Hickories, of which we have eight species, possesses great weight, strength and tenacity, but decays speedily when exposed to heat and moisture, and consequently is unfit for architectural purposes.

GLORY.

How sleep the brave, who sink to rest
By all their country's wishes bless'd:
When Spring, with dewy fingers cold,
Returns to deck their hallow'd mould,
She there shall dress a sweeter sod
Than Fancy's feet have ever trod.

By fairy hands their knell is rung;
By forms unseen their dirge is sung;
There Honour comes, a pilgrim grey,
To bless the turf that wraps their clay;
And Freedom shall awhile repair,
To dwell a weeping hermit there.

COLLINS.

Glory is like a circle in the water,
Which never ceaseth to enlarge itself,
Till by broad spreading, it disperse to nought.

SHAKSPEARE.

Real glory
Springs from the silent conquest of ourselves;
And without that the conqueror is nought
But the first slave.

THOMSON.

OLLY. *Ilex.* Class 4, TETRANDRIA. Order: TETRAGYNIA. The providence of an all-wise Creator is shown in an admirable manner in this beautiful plant. The great hollies which grow in the forest of Needwood bear leaves bristling with thorns to the height of eight or ten feet, and above this height the leaves cease to be thorny. There the plant has no need to arm itself against enemies which cannot reach it. This tree, with its dazzling verdure, is the last ornament of the forests, when they are despoiled by the winter's frosts and chilling blasts; its berries serve as food for the little birds which remain with us through the inclement season of winter; and it also offers them a comfortable shelter amid its foliage.

FORESIGHT.

Some to the holly hedge
Nestling repair, and to the thicket some;
Some to the rude protection of the thorn.

THOMSON.

O reader! hast thou ever stood to see
The holly tree?
The eye that contemplates it well perceives
Its glossy leaves;
Order'd by an Intelligence so wise
As might confound an atheist's sophistries.

Below a circling fence, its leaves are seen
Wrinkled and keen!
No grazing cattle through their prickly round
Can reach to wound;
But, as they grow where nothing is to fear,
Smooth and unarm'd the pointless leaves appear.

SOUTHEY.

OLLYHOCK, or ROSE-MALLOW. *Al-cœa Rosea.* Class 16, MONADELPHIA. Order: POLYANDRIA. All the world knows this superb plant, which is supposed to be a native of China, or rather of Syria, whence it is said to have been brought to Europe in the time of the crusades. From its extreme fecundity in the production of flowers it has been made the emblem of fruitfulness. The Chinese represent nature crowned with its flowers. Pliny mentions it as a rose growing on stalks like the mallow; and Miller states that he received seeds from Istria, where they were gathered in the fields; these seeds produced only single red flowers, while seeds received from Madras yielded plants with double flowers of a variety of colours. H. Smith tells us, that

> From the nectaries of hollyhocks
> The humble bee e'en till he faints will sip.

"There are few flowers that contribute more to the embellishment of large gardens than the hollyhock, although their hardy nature and easy propagation have rendered them so common that they are much less regarded by the generality of florists than they deserve."

FRUITFULNESS.

> But th' earth herself, or her owne motion,
> Out of her *fruitfull* bosome made to growe
> Most daintie trees, that, shooting up anon,
> Did seeme to bow their blooming heads full lowe
> For homage unto her, and like a throne did show.
>
> SPENSER.

> The joyes whereof and happy *fruitfulness,*
> Such as he saw, she gan him lay before,
> And all, though pleasant, yet she made much more.
>
> SPENSER.

ONESTY, or SATIN FLOWER. *Lunaria.* Class 15, TETRADYNAMIA. Order: SILICULOSA. This pretty flower owes its valuable name to the nature of its singular seed-vessel, that honestly shows its number of seeds. *Lunaria,* the botanical name, is derived from *Luna,* the moon, in reference to the shape of its *silique.* Lunaria was formerly used for the most dishonest purposes,

> Enchanting lunary here lies
> In sorceries excelling.
> > DRAYTON.

HONESTY.

An honest soul is like a ship at sea,
That sleeps at anchor when the ocean's calm;
But when she rages, and the wind blows high,
He cuts his way with skill and majesty.
> > BEAUMONT.

An honest man is still an unmoved rock,
Wash'd whiter, but not shaken with the shock;
Whose heart conceives no sinister device;
Fearless he plays with flames, and treads on ice.
> > DAVENPORT.

Take heed what you say, sir,
An hundred honest men! why if there were
So many i' th' city, 't were enough to forfeit
Their charter.
> > SHIRLEY

Heav'n that made me honest, made me more
Than ever king did, when he made a lord.
> > ROWE.

The man who pauses on his honesty
Wants little of the villain.
> > MARTYN.

ONEYSUCKLE, or WOODBINE. *Loni-cera.* Class 5, PENTANDRIA. Order: MoNOGYNIA. The honeysuckle sometimes amorously attaches its pliant branches to the knotted trunk of an ancient oak, and amid the rugged branches of that lordly tree,

The woodbines mix in amorous play,
And breathe their fragrant lives away.

It was said that this feeble tree, thus shooting into the air, would overtop the king of the forest; but, as if its efforts were unavailing, it soon recoiled, and with graceful negligence adorned its friendly supporter with elegant festoons and perfumed garlands.

BONDS OF LOVE.

That sweet honeysuckle, which
Is fair as fragrant.

CARRINGTON.

The woodbine wild,
That loves to hang, on barren boughs remote,
Her wreaths of flowery perfume.

MASON.

Who rears his cot
Deep in the rural shade, and wreaths around
His lattice the rath woodbine!

CARRINGTON.

Fair is thy level landscape, England, fair
As ever nature form'd! Away it sweeps,
A wide, a smiling prospect, gay with flowers,
And waving grass, and trees of amplest growth,
And sparkling rills, and rivers winding slow
Through all the smooth immense. Upon the eye
Arise the village and the village spire,
The clustering hamlet, and the peaceful cot
Clasp'd by the woodbine.

CARRINGTON.

OP. *Humulus.* Class 22, Diœcia. Order: Pentandria. This plant will grow only in rich soils. It is called lupulus by naturalists; and, according to Pliny, was so named because it grew among the willows; to them, by twining round and choking them up, it proved very destructive.

INJUSTICE.

Yes, a most notorious villain;
To see the sufferings of my fellow-creatures,
And own myself a man: to see our senators
Cheat the deluded people with a show
Of liberty, which yet they ne'er must taste of.
They say, by them our hands are free from fetters;
Yet whom they please they lay in basest bonds;
Bring whom they please to infamy and sorrow;
Drive us like wrecks down the rough tide of power,
Whilst no hold's left to save us from destruction:
All that bear this are villains, and I one,
Not to rouse up at the great call of nature,
And check the growth of these domestic spoilers,
That make us slaves, and tell us 't is our charter.
OTWAY.

Justice is lame, as well as blind, amongst us:
The laws, corrupted to their ends that make them,
Serve but for instruments of some new tyranny,
That every day starts up t' enslave us deeper.
OTWAY.

Unheard, the injured orphans now complain;
The widow's cries address the throne in vain,
Causes unjudged disgrace the loaded file,
And sleeping laws the king's neglect revile.
PRIOR.

ORSE CHESTNUT. *Æsculus Hippocasta-num.* Class 7, HEPTANDRIA. Order: MO-NOGYNIA. In the beginning of spring, one rainy day is sufficient to cause this beautiful tree to cover itself with verdure. If it be planted alone, nothing surpasses the ele-gance of its pyramidal form, the beauty of its foliage, or the richness of its flowers, which sometimes make it appear as an immense lustre or chandelier, all covered with pearls. Fond of ostentation and richness, it covers with flowers the grass which it overshadows, and yields to the idler a most delightful shade. To the poor man it is of little service, sup-plying him with nothing more than a light and porous timber, and a bitter fruit. Naturalists and physicians have attributed to this child of Asia a thousand good qualities which it does not possess.

LUXURY.

It is a shame, that man, that has the seeds
Of virtue in him, springing unto glory,
Should make his soul degenerous with sin,
And slave to luxury; to drown his spirits
In lees of sloth; to yield up the weak day
To wine, to lust, and banquets.

MARMYON.

War destroys men, but luxury mankind
At once corrupts; the body and the mind.

CROWN.

Fell luxury! more perilous to youth
Than storms or quicksands, poverty or chains.

MORE.

Sofas 't was half a sin to sit upon,
So costly were they; carpets, every stitch
Of workmanship so rare, they made you wish
You could glide o'er them like a golden fish.

BYRON.

OUSELEEK. *Sempervivum Tectorum.* Class 11, DODECANDRIA. Order: DODECA-GYNIA. The Houseleek is made the emblem of vivacity, because it retains its vivacious nature even on the hot tiles of cottage roofs. In such situations it generally bespeaks the residence of some good old dame well skilled in simples, and reposing implicit faith in their efficacy.

VIVACITY.

The sprightly Sylvia trips along the green;
She runs, but hopes she does not run unseen.
POPE.

Tower'd cities please us then,
And the busy haunts of men,
Where throngs of knights and barons bold,
In weeds of peace, high triumphs hold;
With store of ladies, whose bright eyes
Rain influence, and judge the prize
Of wit or arms, while both contend
To win her grace whom all commend.
There let Hymen oft appear
In saffron robe with taper clear,
And pomp and feast and revelry,
With mask and antique pageantry;
Such sights as youthful poets dream
On summer eves by haunted stream,
Then to the well-trod stage anon,
If Jonson's learned sock be on,
Or sweetest Shakspeare, Fancy's child,
Warble his native wood-notes wild.
MILTON.

YACINTH. *Hyacinthus.* Class 6, HEX-ANDRIA. Order: MONOGYNIA. The hyacinth, so celebrated in the songs of the poets, from the time of Homer to the present day, is made emblematical of games, or play, in allusion to the fabulous origin of this flower, which, according to mythologists, sprang from the blood of Hyacinthus, who was killed by a quoit, through the agency of Zephyr, who blew it from its course as it passed from the hand of Apollo, and smote the unfortunate youth on the head. Hurd mentions

> The melancholy hyacinth that weeps
> All night, and never lifts an eye all day;

probably in allusion to the melancholy fate of Hyacinthus.

PLAY.

Oh! mournful, graceful, sapphire-colour'd flower,
  That keep'st thine eye for ever fix'd on earth!
  Gentle and sad, a foe thou seem'st to mirth —
What secret sorrow makes thee thus to lower?

Perhaps 't is that thy place thou canst not change,
  And thou art pining at thy prison'd lot;
  But oh! where couldst thou find a sweeter spot,
Wert thou permitted earth's wide bounds to range?

In pensive grove, meet temple for thy form,
  Where, with her silvery music, doth intrude
  The lucid stream, where nought unkind or rude
Durst break of harmony the hallow'd charm.

Thy beauties, all unseen by vulgar eyes,
  Sol, in his brightness, still delights to view;
  He clothes thy petals in his glorious hue,
To show how much of old he did thee prize.

ANON.

YDRANGER. *Hydrangea Hortensis.* Class 10, DECANDRIA. Order: DIGYNIA. The Chinese Guelder Rose is presented as an emblem of a boaster, because its magnificent flowers are never succeeded by a fruit, thus resembling the vaunting words of a braggadocia which are not followed by suitable results. It is a native of China and Japan, where it is cultivated in gardens. It was brought to England by Sir Joseph Banks in 1790.

BOASTER.

The honour is overpaid,
When he that did the act is commentator.
SHIRLEY.

He that vaunts
Of a received favour, ought to be
Punish'd as sacrilegious persons are,
'Cause he doth violate that sacred thing,
Pure, spotless honour.
CARTWRIGHT.

I'll turn two mincing steps
Into a manly stride: and speak of frays
Like a fine bragging youth; and tell quaint lies
How honourable ladies sought my love,
Which I denying, they fell sick and died:
I could not do with all: — then I will repent,
And wish, for all that, that I had not kill'd them,
And twenty of these puny lies I'll tell,
That men shall swear I have discontinued school
Above a twelvemonth.
SHAKSPEARE.

We rise in glory, as we sink in pride;
Where boasting ends, there dignity begins.
YOUNG.

CE PLANT. *Mesembryanthemum Crys-tallinum.* Class 12, ICOSANDRIA. Order: PENTAGYNIA. The leaves of this singular plant are covered with transparent vesicles full of water. When in the shade it seems to be gemmed with dew-drops; but when exposed to the burning sun, it appears scat-tered over with frozen crystals, which reflect with great bril-liancy the rays of the sun; on this account it is commonly called ice plant.

YOUR LOOKS FREEZE ME.

With pellucid studs the ice-flower gems
His rising foliage, and his candied stems.

DARWIN.

Tell me, perhaps thou think'st in that sweet look
The white is beauty's native tapestry?
'T is crystal, friend, *iced* in the frozen sea.

FLETCHER.

Be she constant, be she fickle,
Be she fire, or be she *ice.*

COTTON.

Those glances work on me like the weak shine
The frosty sun throws on the Appenine,
When the hills' active coldness doth go near
To freeze the glimmering taper to his sphere.

BEAUMONT.

Then, taught both impudence and wit,
I singled out my foe, used all the arts
That love could think upon, and in the end
Found a most absolute repulse.

SHIRLEY.

CELAND MOSS. *Cetraria Islandica.* Class 24, CRYPTOGAMIA. Order: LICHENES. Lichens are valuable for their own uses, as well as being such good settlers in barren ground to make it fit for other residents. One of the most useful lichens is that known by the name of Iceland Moss, which is plentiful with us, though not sufficiently so to supply the shops, now that it has become a fashionable remedy for coughs, consumptions, and the like. Great quantities are sent here from Norway and Iceland, where, and in Lapland, it is much used as an article of food; they either eat it boiled in broth or milk, or after the bitter properties are extracted, it is dried and made into bread.

HEALTH.

Ah! what avail the largest gifts of heaven,
When drooping health and spirits go amiss?
How tasteless then whatever can be given?
Health is the vital principle of bliss,
And exercise of health. In proof of this,
Behold the wretch who slugs his life away,
Soon swallow'd in disease's sad abyss;
While he whom toil has braced, or manly play,
Has light as air each limb, each thought as clear as day.

O who can speak the vigorous joys of health!
Unclogg'd the body, unobscured the mind:
The morning rises gay; with pleasing stealth,
The temperate evening falls serene and kind.
In health the wiser brutes true gladness find.
See how the younglings frisk along the meads,
As May comes on and wakes the balmy wind;
Rampant with life, their joy all joy exceeds:
Yet what but high-strung health this dancing pleasaunce
    breeds?
                                        THOMSON.

NDIAN CRESS, THREE-COLOURED. *Tropseolum Tricolorum.* Class 8, OCTAN-DRIA. Order: MONOGYNIA. This elegant plant is a native of Valparaiso; from whence it was introduced in 1828. The striking distinction and unrivalled brilliancy in the colours of the flowers render this one of the most desirable of climbing plants. The gentle drooping of the flowers have occasioned its adoption as an emblem of Resignation.

RESIGNATION.

Passing the inclosure where the dead repose,
  I saw, in sable weeds, a gentle pair
Lingering with fond regard at evening's close,
  Beside a little grave fresh swelling there:

Silent they stood—serene their thoughtful air;
  There fell no tear, no vain complaint arose;
Faith seem'd to prompt the unutterable prayer,
  And to their view the eternal home disclose.

Next Sabbath brought me where the flow'ret lay,
  Record of high descent the marble bore,
Heir of a noble house and only stay:
  And these words gather'd from the Bible's store—
'The Lord hath given, the Lord hath ta'en away,
  His holy name be blessed evermore.'

ANON.

You shall be as a father to my youth,
My voice shall sound as you do prompt mine ear;
And I will stoop and humble my intents
To your well-practised, wise directions.

SHAKSPEARE.

My other self, my counsel's consistory,
My oracle, my prophet!—My dear cousin,
I, as a child, will go by thy direction.

SHAKSPEARE.

RIS. *Iris.* Class 3, TRIANDRIA. Order: MONOGYNIA. This plant is supposed to have been named after Juno's attendant, because its colours are similar to those bestowed on the messenger of that goddess, by poets and mythological writers. Iris is usually portrayed as descending from a rainbow; and the eye of heaven (Plutarch says that is the meaning of the word Iris) is not more variegated than the flower that has been honoured by her name.

MESSAGE.

All with their pearls so fair,
The gay flowers wreathed were,
  But, 'midst them all,
Crown'd at the rainbow festival,
A sapphire-colour'd blossom shone
The loveliest there; no other one
  Her jewels wore
So gracefully. Her robe all o'er
Was radiant, yet deep blue, like twilight sky,
And softly shaded, as when clouds do lie
Upon the deep expanse. 'T was strange, none knew
A name for this fair form, so bright and blue:
But sister-flowrets fancifully said,
As they to note her beauty had been led
By its enhancement in the rainbow shower,
They e'en would call her IRIS from that hour.

TWAMLEY.

Iris, on saffron wings array'd with dew
Of various colours, through the sunbeams flew.

VIRGIL.

VY. *Hedera.* Class 5, PENTANDRIA. Order: MONOGYNIA. Faithful love secures with a branch of ivy the quickly fading roses which adorn the brow. Friendship has chosen for its device an ivy which clothes a fallen tree, with these words:—"*Rien ne peut m'en détacher.*" In Greece, the altar of Hymen was surrounded with ivy, a sprig of which was presented by the priest to a new-married spouse, as the symbol of an indissoluble knot. The Bacchantes, old Silenus, and Bacchus himself were crowned with ivy. Ingratitude has sometimes been represented by ivy, as when it attaches itself to a young tree it confines the stem, and consequently prevents the free circulation of the sap. The author of a French work has repelled this calumny. The ivy appears to him to be the emblem of eternal friendship; he says, "Nothing is able to separate the ivy from the tree around which it has once entwined itself; it clothes the object with its own foliage in that inclement season when its black boughs are covered with hoar frost; the companion of its destinies, it falls when the tree is cut down. Death itself does not detach it, but it continues to decorate with its constant verdure the dry trunk it had chosen as its support.

FRIENDSHIP.

Though long the time since I my friend have seen,
Though long to me his tongue hath silent been,
Though absence, distance, and diverse pursuit
Might seem to aim at Friendship's vig'rous root,
Yet is the plant too tough to own the pow'r
Of life's poor, changing, transitory hour.
No! Friendship is a plant of heavenly birth,
Constant its nature, and immense its worth,
Its essence virtue, and is known to rest
And glow most warmly in the virtuous breast!

PRATTENT

ASMINE, WHITE. *Jasminum Officinale.* Class 2, DIANDRIA. Order: MONOGYNIA. Though born beneath a summer sky, and nourished by a kindlier soil than ours, yet the pure, the fragrant, the modest, maidenly Jasmine has become unto us as an old familiar friend, and is now as well known, and as frequently seen climbing round the cottage-porch, as our own .scious Honey-suckle.

AMIABILITY.

The free and sportive *Jasmine-tree!*
  O'er the lone captive's darksome cell,
How many a tale of liberty
  Could'st thou to his sad spirit tell!
Each slender tendril floating there,
  Laughing in sunshine, nursed by showers,
And gemming the perfumed air
  With winged wreaths of starry flowers.

The captive saw the Jasmine-tree,
  Whose slight and fragile branches crept
Through the dim loop-hole steadily—
  He sadly gazed on them, and wept;
Each wandering breeze their light leaves stirr'd,
  They look'd up to the glorious sky,
And, poised upon them, many a bird
  Trill'd forth its free wild melody.

Perchance there grew a Jasmine-tree
  Beside his own ancestral hall,
Where he had loved, in childhood's glee,
  To watch its short-lived blossoms fall:
Alas! how soon those blossoms died,
  When sever'd from their native stem!
Did not like early doom betide
  That captive! Drooped he not like them?
                                        TWAMLEY.

ASMINE, CAROLINA YELLOW. *Gelsimium Nitidum.* Class 5, **Pentandria.** Order: **Digynia.** This beautiful flower grows wild in great abundance in our southern states, spreading over the hedges and trees and shedding a most delicious fragrance. It is a favourite of the Humming-Bird, and a British writer regrets that in transferring it to England it is necessary to separate it from the sprightly and elegant little bird, who finds sustenance in the nectareous vessels of its flowers.

SEPARATION.

When the tree of Love is budding first,
    Ere yet its leaves are green,
Ere yet, by shower and sunbeam nurst
    Its infant life has been;
The wild bee's slightest touch might wring
    The buds from off the tree,
As the gentle dip of the swallow's wing
    Breaks the bubbles on the sea.

But when its open leaves have found
    A home in the free air,
Pluck them, and there remains a wound
    That ever rankles there.
The blight of hope and happiness
    Is felt when fond ones part,
And the bitter tear that follows is
    The life-blood of the heart.

Halleck.

Let's not unman each other—part at once:
All farewells should be sudden, when for ever,
Else they make an eternity of moments,
And clog the last sad sands of life with tears.

Byron.

ONQUIL. *Narcissus Jonquilla.* Class 6, HEXANDRIA. Order: MONOGYNIA. This species of narcissus is distinguished from others by its rush-like foliage; hence its name, derived from *juncus*, rushy. It is more fragrant than any other species of the plant, and is frequently found too strong for moderate-sized rooms. It flowers well in water, is of great beauty, and very popular.

DESIRE.

    Nor gradual bloom is wanting,
Nor hyacinths of purest virgin white,
Low bent and blushing inward; nor jonquils
Of potent fragrance.

THOMSON.

O fierce desire, the spring of sighs and tears,
Relieved with want, impoverish'd with store,
Nurst with vain hopes, and fed with doubtful fears,
Whose force withstood, increaseth more and more!

BRANDON.

'T is most ignoble, that a mind unshaken
By fear, should by a vain desire be broken;
Or that those powers no labour e'er could vanquish,
Should be o'ercome and thrall'd by sordid pleasure.

CHAPMAN.

Thou blind man's mark; thou fool's self-chosen snare,
Fond fancy's scum, and dregs of scatter'd thoughts;
Band of all evils; cradle of causeless care;
Thou web of ill, whose end is never wrought;
Desire! Desire! I have too dearly bought
With price of mangled mind thy worthless ware,
Too long, too long, asleep thou hast me brought,
Who shouldst my mind to higher things prepare.

SIDNEY.

UNIPER. *Juniperus.* Class 22, Diœcia. Order: Monadelphia. The ancients consecrated this shrub to the Eumenides. The smoke of its green branches was the incense which, in preference, they chose to offer to the infernal gods; and burnt its berries, on funeral occasions, to drive away evil spirits. The simple villagers of England superstitiously believe that the perfume of its berries purifies the air, and protects them from the malevolence of wicked genii.

The Chinese delight to decorate their gardens with this plant. It groups and combines very well with cypresses, American cedars, and various species of the pine and fir tribe. It is commonly found growing wild on the outskirts of woods and forests, where it often affords a safe retreat to the hunted hare, which, in the last extremity, conceals itself beneath its protecting branches. It is said that the powerful odour emitted by this plant defeats the keen scent of the hound.

Its thick branches, bristling with thorns, are covered with thousands of brilliant insects, which seem to imagine this tree is provided as a protection for their weakness.

ASYLUM. PROTECTION.

Welcome, pure thoughts; welcome, ye silent groves;
These guests, these courts, my soul most dearly loves.
Now the wing'd people of the sky shall sing
My cheerful anthems to the gladsome spring:
A prayer-book now shall be my looking-glass,
In which I will adore sweet virtue's face.
Here dwell no hateful looks, no palace cares,
No broken vows dwell here, nor pale-faced fears:
Then here I'll sit, and sigh my lost love's folly,
And learn to affect an holy melancholy;
   And if contentment be a stranger then,
   I'll ne'er look for it, but in heaven again.

Anon.

ENNEDIA, ELEGANT SCARLET. *Kennedia Coccinea Elegans.* Class DIADELPHIA. Order: DECANDRIA. This is a charming variety of the *Kennedia Coccinea*, and deserves the most extensive cultivation. It grows delicate, and is well suited for climbing up a pillar in a conservatory, where it will flower to perfection. Its rare delicacy and beauty render it a suitable emblem of Mental Beauty.

MENTAL BEAUTY.

When I approach
Her loveliness, so absolute she seems,
And in herself complete, so well to know
Her own, that what she wills to do or say,
Seems wisest, virtuousest, discreetest, best,
All higher knowledge in her presence falls
Degraded, wisdom in discourse with her
Loses discount'nanced, and like folly shows.

MILTON.

What is beauty ? Not the show
Of shapely limbs and features. No.
These are but flowers,
That have their dated hours,
To breathe their momentary sweets, then go.
'T is the stainless soul within
That outshines the fairest skin.

HUNT.

Mark her majestic fabric ! she 's a temple
Sacred by birth, and built by hands divine ;
Her soul 's the deity that lodges there ;
Nor is the pile unworthy of the god.

DRYDEN.

ARKSPUR. *Delphinium Ajacis.* Class 13, POLYANDRIA. Order: PENTAGYNIA. Found in Europe, Siberia and America, and called Larkspur from a fancied resemblance in the horn-shaped nectary at the back of the corolla to the spur of the Lark's foot.

ARDENT ATTACHMENT.

Helen, I love thee; by my life, I do;
I swear by that which I will lose for thee,
To prove him false, that says I love thee not.

SHAKSPEARE.

O happy fair!
Your eyes are load-stars, and your tongue's sweet air,
More tunable than lark to shepherd's ear,
When wheat is green, when hawthorn buds appear.

SHAKSPEARE.

O, gentle Romeo,
If thou dost love, pronounce it faithfully.
Or if thou think'st I am too quickly won,
I'll frown, and be perverse, and say thee nay,
So thou wilt woo: but, else, not for the world.

SHAKSPEARE.

In truth, fair Montague, I am too fond;
And therefore thou may'st think my 'haviour light:
But trust me, gentleman, I'll prove more true
Than those that have more cunning.

SHAKSPEARE.

Sweet, good night!
This bud of love, by summer's ripening breath,
May prove a beauteous flower when next we meet.

SHAKSPEARE.

AUREL. *Prunus Laurocerasus.* Class 12, Icosandria. Order: Monogynia. To wear the crown of laurel, has been the soldier's ambition from the earliest ages to the present day; it is also regarded as the appropriate reward of poets, orators, and philosophers.

GLORY.

The *laurel*, meed of mighty conquerors.
Spenser.

Their temples wreath'd with leaves that still renew:
For deathless *laurel* is the victor's due.
Dryden.

Real *glory*
Springs from the conquest of ourselves;
And without that the conqueror is nought
But the first slave.
Thomson.

And should the aspiring man, that makes his gain
Of others' hurts, not hurt himself for gain?
Not, when he stabs another for a purse,
Prick his own bosom for a dearer price,
And wound his heart, to *laurel-crown* his head.
Bird.

Brave though we fall, and honour'd if we live,
Or let us *glory* gain, or *glory* give.
Pope.

And glory long has made the sages smile;
'T is something, nothing, words, illusion, wind—
Depending more upon the historian's style
Than on the name a person leaves behind.
Byron.

AUREL, MOUNTAIN. *Rhododendron.* Class 10, DECANDRIA. Order: MONOGYNIA. This beautiful tree is found in North America, Siberia, Europe, and the western part of Asia. It is cultivated in the United States as an ornament to gardens and grounds.

AMBITION.

How dost thou wear and weary out thy days,
Restless *Ambition,* never at an end.

DANIEL.

A funerale stone
Or verse, I covet none;
But only crave
Of you that I may have
A sacred laurel springing from my grave;
Which being seen
Blest with perpetual greene,
May grow to be
Not so much call'd a tree,
As the eternal monument of me.

HERRICK.

I have ventured,
Like little wanton boys that swim on bladders,
This many summers in a sea of glory:
But far beyond my depth: my high-blown pride
At length broke under me; and now has left me,
Weary, and old with service, to the mercy
Of a rude stream, that must for ever hide me.

SHAKSPEARE.

Cromwel, I charge thee, fling away ambition:
By that sin fell the angels; how can man then,
The image of his Maker, hope to win by't?

SHAKSPEARE.

 AURUSTINUS. *Viburnum Tinus.* Class 5, Pentandria. Order: Trigynia. This is one of the prettiest of evergreen shrubs, and is the gift of Spain to our highly favoured land. In winter it is the ornament of our groves, displaying its shining leaves and showy white flowers when other trees have ceased to bloom.

Neither the hot breath of summer nor the cold kiss of winter can rob it of its charms; but to preserve it we must tend it with assiduous care. The symbol of a constant and delicate friendship, it ever seeks to please, yet dies if neglected.

I DIE IF NEGLECTED.

He does not love me!
I never dream'd of this! To be his bride
Was all the Heav'n I look'd for! Not to love me
When I have been ten years affianced to him!—
When I have lived for him—shut up my heart,
With every pulse and hope, for his use only—
Worshipp'd—oh God! idolatrously loved him!
. . . .
Why has he sought to marry me? Why still
Renew the broken pledge my father made him?
Why, for ten years, with war and policy,
Strive for my poor alliance? . . . . . .
. . . . He *must* love me,
Or l shall break my heart! I never had
One other hope in life! I never link'd
One thought, but to this chain! I have no blood—
No breath—no being—separate from Sforza!
Nothing has any other name! The sun
Shined like his smile—the lightning was his glory.

WILLIS.

 ILAC, PERSIAN. *Syringa.* Class 2, DI-ANDRIA. Order: MONOGYNIA. This more delicate variety of the lilac is becoming a favourite among the florists. It is made the emblem of the first emotions of Love, on account of its delicacy, both of fragrance and colour.

FIRST EMOTIONS OF LOVE.

We sat and sigh'd,
And look'd upon each other, and conceived
Not what we ail'd; yet something we did ail;
And yet were well, and yet we were not well:
And what was our disease we could not tell:
Then would we kiss, then sigh, then look: And thus
In that first garden of our simpleness
We spent our childhood: But when years began
To reap the fruit of knowledge; ah, how then
Would she with graver looks, with sweet stern brow,
Check my presumption, and my forwardness!
Yet still would give me flow'rs; still would she show
What she would have me, yet not have me know.
DANIEL.

She felt his flame; but deep within her breast,
In bashful coyness, or in maiden pride,
The soft return conceal'd; save when it stole
In sidelong glances from her downcast eye,
Or from her swelling soul in stifled sighs.
THOMSON.

What is this subtle searching flame of love,
That penetrates the tender breast unmask'd,
And blasts the heart of adamant within;
As the quick light'ning oft calcines the blade
Of temper'd steel, and leaves the sheath unhurt.
DARCY.

ILY, SUPERB. *Lilium Superbum.* Class 6, HEXANDRIA. Order: MONOGYNIA. The stem is erect, straight, six feet high, supporting a most superb pyramid of light orange-coloured flowers, sometimes to the number of forty. This species is occasionally seen in our gardens, improved by cultivation.

SPLENDOUR.

Nor are thy evening splendours, mighty Orb!
  Less beautiful: and oh! more touching far,
And of more power thought, feeling to absorb
  In silent ecstasy, to me they are;
When, watchful of thy exit, one pale star
  Shines on the brow of summer's loveliest eve;
And breezes, softer than the soft guitar,
  Whose plaintive notes Castilian maids deceive,
Among the foliage sigh, and take of thee their leave.

Oh! then it is delightful to behold
  Thy calm departure; soothing to survey
Through opening clouds, by thee all edged with gold,
  The milder pomp of thy declining sway:
How beautiful, on church-tower old and grey,
  Is shed thy parting smile; how brightly glow
Thy last beams on some tall tree's loftiest spray,
  While silvery mists half veil the trunk below,
And hide the rippling stream that scarce is heard to flow!
                                        BARTON.

O place and greatness, millions of false eyes
Are stuck upon thee! volumes of report
Run with these false and most contrarious guests
Upon thy doings! thousand 'scapes of wit
Make thee the father of their idle dream,
And rack thee in their fancies.
                                        SHAKSPEARE.

ILY, YELLOW. Class 6, HEXANDRIA.
Order: MONOGYNIA. This flower is a native of Persia, transferred to Europe, and
thence to the United States. The flowers
of this plant speedily fade, seldom conti-
nuing two days in bloom; for this reason it
has been assigned as the emblem of co-
quetry. As an equivalent for the transient duration of its flowers, it displays its beauty by a continual succession of blossom,
and gives out for some time a very agreeable odour; and this the
more powerfully when planted in shady or moist situations.

COQUETRY.

A beam upon the myrtle fell
　　From dewy evening's purest sky,
'T was like the glance I love so well,
　　Dear Eva, from thy moonlight eye.

I look'd around the summer grove,
　　On every tree its lustre shone;
For all had felt that look of love
　　The silly myrtle deem'd its own.

Eva! behold thine image there,
　　As fair, as false thy glances fall;
But who the worthless smile would share
　　That sheds its light alike on all.

DRAKE.

Nymph of the mincing mouth and languid eye,
And lisping tongue so soft, and head awry,
And flutt'ring heart, of leaves of aspen made;
Who were thy parents, blushful virgin? — say;
Perchance dame Folly gave thee to the day,
With Gaffer Ignorance's aid.

WOLCOT.

 ILY OF THE VALLEY. *Convallaria majalis.* Class 6, HEXANDRIA. Order: MoNOGYNIA. This lowly plant loves the shelter of the hollow valleys, the shade of oaks, or the cool banks of streams.

The "Naiad-like lily of the vale, whose tremulous bells are seen through their pavilions of tender green," should form a part of every wreath that crowns the happy, the innocent and the gay.

Keats has assigned a diadem to this lowly plant: —

> No flower amid the garden fairer grows
> Than the sweet lily of the lowly vale,
> The queen of flowers.

RETURN OF HAPPINESS.

That white hand is withdrawn, that fair, sad face is gone;
But the music of that silver voice is flowing sweetly on,—
Not, as of late, with cheerful tones, but mournfully and low,—
A ballad of a tender maid heart-broken long ago,
Of him who died in battle, the youthful and the brave,
And her who died of sorrow upon his early grave.

But see, along that rugged path, a fiery horseman ride;
See the torn plume, the tarnish'd belt, the sabre at his side;
His spurs are in his horse's sides, his hand casts loose the rein;
There's sweat upon the streaming flank, and foam upon the
    mane;
He speeds toward that olive bower, along the shaded hill:
God shield the hapless maiden there, if he should mean her ill.

And suddenly the song has ceased, and suddenly I hear
A shriek sent up amid the shade—a shriek—but not of fear;
For tender accents follow, and tenderer pauses speak
The overflow of gladness when words are all too weak:
"I lay my good sword at thy feet, for now Peru is free,
And I am come to dwell beside the olive grove with thee."

BRYANT.

 ILY. *Lilium Candidum.* Class 6, HEX-
ANDRIA. Order: MONOGYNIA. All nations
agree in making this flower the symbol of
purity and modesty; and its beauty and delicacy have ever been the theme of admiration with the poets, from the time of Solo-
mon to the present day.

PURITY AND MODESTY.

Where may the bright flower be met
That can match with Margaret,—
Margaret, stately, staid, and good,
Growing up to womanhood:
Loving, thoughtful, wise, and kind,
Pure in heart and strong in mind?
Eyes deep blue as is the sky
When the full moon sails on high;
Eye-brow true and forehead fair,
And dark, richly-braided hair,
And a queenly head well set,
Crown my maiden Margaret.
Where's the flower that thou canst find
Match for her in form and mind?

Fair *white lilies*, having birth
In their native genial earth;—
These in scent and queenly grace,
Match thy maiden's form and face!

HOWITT.

Observe the rising lily's snowy grace;
Observe the various vegetable race;
They neither toil nor spin, but careless grow;
Yet, see how warm they blush! how bright they glow!
What regal vestments can with them compare?
What king so shining, or what queen so fair?

THOMSON.

INDEN TREE. *Tilia.* Class 15, POLY-
ANDRIA. Order: MONOGYNIA. Baucis was
changed into the Linden tree, which has
ever since been the emblem of conjugal
love. In glancing over the consecrated
plants in the mythology of the ancients, we
cannot fail to admire their fitness to represent the various qualities of which they are symbolical.

Beauty—grace—simplicity—an extreme softness of manner,
and an innocent gaiety, should be, in all ages, the properties and
accomplishments of a tender wife. We find all these qualities
united in the Linden tree; which, in spring, is ever covered with
a soft and delicate verdure, and exhales a very delightful fragrance, while it lavishes the honey of its flowers upon the busy
bee.

CONJUGAL LOVE.

Are we not one? are we not join'd by heav'n?
Each interwoven with the other's fate?
Are we not mix'd like streams of meeting rivers,
Whose blended waters are no more distinguished,
But roll into the sea one common flood?
ROWE.

Oh speak the joy! ye whom the sudden tear
Surprises often, when you look around,
And nothing strikes the eye but sights of bliss,
All various nature pressing on the heart,
And elegant sufficiency, content;
Retirement, rural quiet, friendship, books,
Ease and alternate labour, useful life,
Progressive virtue, and approving heaven.
These are the matchless joys of virtuous love;
And thus their moments fly.
THOMSON.

Domestic happiness, thou only bliss
Of paradise that has survived the fall!
COWPER.

IVE OAK. *Quercus virens.* Class 21, MONŒCIA. Order: POLYANDRIA. The Live Oak is found from 37° to Florida, and westward to the mouth of the Sabine river, but never more than 15 or 20 miles from the sea. It attains the height of 40 or 45 feet, with a trunk a foot or two in diameter, but is sometimes much larger. The wood is the finest material we have for ship-building, is much stronger and more durable than the White Oak, and, indeed, is said to be no way inferior to the European species. In consequence of its narrow limits and the more profitable culture of Cotton in the districts where it abounds, its total extinction is considered certain at no distant day.

LIBERTY.

O *Liberty!* with profitless endeavour
Have I pursued thee, many a weary hour;
  But thou nor swell'st the victor's strain, nor ever
Didst breathe thy soul in forms of human power.
  Alike from all, howe'er they praise thee,
  (Not prayer, nor boastful name delays thee,)
    Alike from Priestcraft's harpy minions,
  And factious Blasphemy's obscener slaves;
    Thou speedest on thy subtle pinions,
The guide of homeless winds, and playmate of the waves!
And there I felt thee!—on that sea-cliff's verge,
  Whose pines, scarce travell'd by the breeze above,
Had made one murmur with the distant surge!
Yes, while I stood and gazed, my temples bare,
And shot my being through earth, sea, and air,
  Possessing all things with intensest love
    O Liberty! my spirit felt thee there.

COLERIDGE.

The love of liberty with life is given,
And life itself th' inferior gift of heaven.

DRYDEN.

OBELIA. *Lobelia Fulgens.* Class 5, PENT-ANDRIA. Order: MONOGYNIA. Of the genus Lobelia there are nearly one hundred species, most of them indigenous in America, South Africa, and Australasia. One of the species has obtained great notoriety in consequence of its being applied to the purposes of the Thompsonian practitioners in medicine.

ARROGANCE.

With proud disdain how she uprears her stem,
          Unbending, tall;
As if she arrogantly, vainly said —
          "What are ye all,
Pale, paltry buds, that trail and creep around,
Scarce rising from the base and sordid ground?

See how the butterflies, with gay-plumed wings
          On me alight —
Attracted by my tow'ring, stately stem,
          And colours bright —
None in *my* presence cast a thought on you —
Their homage paid to me, away they go."

So seem'd this gaudy flower to discourse
          Unto the fair,
Humble, and lowly buds, which all around
          Disposed were;
And much her scorn on their mean rank was bent;
Which scorns howe'er brought them no discontent.
                              TWAMLEY.

He that is proud eats up himself. Pride is
His own glass, his own trumpet, his own chronicle;
And whatever praises itself but in
The deed, devours the deed in the praise.
                              SHAKSPEARE.

OCUST. *Robinia pseudacacia.* Class **17**, DIADELPHIA. Order: DECANDRIA. The Locust is found native in the valleys of the Alleghanies, and throughout the Western States, but everywhere mixed with the other trees, not occupying exclusively the soil, even of limited districts. It is now planted about houses in all parts of the Union, as it has a rapid growth, but unfortunately it is very generally liable to injury from the attacks of an insect (Callidium flexuosum). The wood is superior to that of most trees of northern climates. It is much sought for in naval architecture, and is substituted for box by turners: for trunnels it is used almost exclusively.

VICISSITUDE.

The flower that smiles to-day
　To-morrow dies;
All that we wish to stay,
　Tempts, and then flies:
What is this world's delight? —
Lightning that mocks the night,
Brief even as bright.

Virtue, how frail it is!
　Friendship, too rare!
Love, how it sells poor bliss
　For proud despair!
But we, though soon they fall,
Survive their joy, and all
Which ours we call.

Whilst skies are blue and bright,
　Whilst flowers are gay,
Whilst eyes that change ere night
　Make glad the day;
Whilst yet the calm hours creep,
Dream thou: — and from thy sleep
Then wake to weep! SHELLEY.

ONDON PRIDE. *Saxifraga Umbrosa.*
Class 10, DECANDRIA. Order: DIGYNIA.
This pretty and almost universal border
plant, is a species of saxifrage. It has received the name also of none-so-pretty;
and, if we view it with attention, we shall
acknowledge that its prettily spotted petals,
which are painted with so much delicacy, fully deserve this
appellation. Notwithstanding its beauty, it has been made the
emblem of a light and frivolous sentiment, for a lover would
think it an insult to his mistress, to present her with a nosegay
of its flowers.

FRIVOLITY.

Around him some mysterious circle thrown
Repell'd approach and show'd him still alone;
Upon his eye sat something of reproof,
That kept at least *frivolity* aloof.

BYRON.

His sports were fair, his joyance innocent,
Sweet without sour, and honey without gall;
And he himself seem'd made for merriment,
Merrily masking both in bower and hall.

SPENSER.

Where is his son,
The nimble-footed, mad-cap prince of Wales,
And his comrades, that doff'd the world aside,
And bid it pass.

SHAKSPEARE.

To business that we love, we rise betime,
And go to it with delight.

SHAKSPEARE.

Strike up the dance, the cava bowl fill high,
Drain every drop! — to-morrow we may die.

BYRON.

OTOS. *Lotus.* Class 17, Diadelphia. Order: Decandria. A favourite plant among the ancients, who frequently refer to it in their poetry and mythology. The definition of Lotos in the Greek Lexicon, says Mrs. Wirt, is this, "A tree whose fruit is so sweet that foreigners, having tasted of it, forget their own country"—whence the proverb, to have eaten of the Lotos, is applied to those who prefer a foreign country to their own.

Its flower is the emblem of *estranged love;* its leaf of *recantation.*

ESTRANGED LOVE.

That anxious torture may I never feel,
Which, doubtful, watches o'er a wandering heart.
O who that bitter torment can reveal,
Or tell the pining anguish of that smart!
In those affections may I ne'er have part,
Which easily transferr'd can learn to rove:
No, dearest Cupid! when I feel thy dart,
For thy sweet Psyche's sake may no false love,
The tenderness I prize lightly from me rove!

Tighe.

In want, and war, and peril,
Things that would thrill the hearer's blood to tell of,
My heart grew human when I thought of thee —
Imogine would have shudder'd for my danger —
Imogine would have bound my leechless wounds —
Imogine would have sought my nameless corse —
And known it well — and she was wedded — wedded —
Was there no name in hell's dark catalogue
To brand thee with, but mine immortal foe's?
And did I 'scape from war, and want, and famine,
To perish by the falsehood of a woman.

Maturin.

UCERN. *Medicago Sativa.* Class 17, Diadelphia. Order: Decandria. Lucern occupies the same ground for a long period, but when it forsakes it, it is for ever. On this account it has been made the emblem of life. Nothing is more charming than a field of lucern in full flower. It seems spread before our eyes like a carpet of green and violet. Cherished by the husbandman, it yields him an abundant crop without much care; and, when mowed, it springs up again. The cattle rejoice at its appearance; it is a favourite plant with the sheep; and the goat receives it as a delicacy; while the horse also eats it with avidity.

LIFE.

Catch then, O catch the transient hour,
Improve each moment as it flies;
Life's a short summer — man a flower,
He dies — alas! how soon he dies!

Johnson.

Reflect that life and death, affecting sounds,
Are only varied modes of endless being,
Reflect that life, like every other blessing,
Derives its value from its use alone;
Not for itself but for a nobler end
Th' Eternal gave it, and that end is virtue.
When inconsistent with the greater good,
Reason commands to cast the less away;
Thus life, with loss of wealth, is well preserved,
And virtue cheaply saved with loss of life.

Johnson.

'Tis but a night, a long and moonless night;
We make the grave our bed, and then are gone.

Blair.

ADWORT, ROCK. *Asperugo*. Class **5**, PENTANDRIA. Order: MONOGYNIA. This plant was esteemed by the ancients on account of its supposed power to allay anger. The species generally are showy plants, and of easy culture. The rock madwort is **very** ornamental early in the season.

TRANQUILLITY.

Wilt thou go far away from this dark world with **me**,
To an isle of our own, in a warm sunny sea,
Where summer lives on, in a soft genial clime,
And breathes the rich fragrance of orange and lime?

Wilt thou go with me, love! where the halcyon hours
Are noiseless as angels, that move among flowers,
Where care may not come to disturb our repose,
As the calm tide of pleasure unsulliedly flows?

The music that comes on the citron-gale's wing
Shall wake thee at morn, and new happiness bring,
And evening shall find thee, with innocence gay,
Living over in dreams all the joys of the day.

The bark is unmoor'd that shall bear us away,
And the fresh-blowing breeze only chides our delay;
Then haste, ere the summer of youth has gone by,
To our island of love with its warm sunny sky!

DAWES.

      All is gentle: nought
Stirs rudely; but congenial with the night,
Whatever walks is gliding like a spirit.

BYRON.

AGNOLIA, LAUREL-LEAVED. *Magnolia Grandiflora.* Class 13, POLYANDRIA. Order: POLYGYNIA. This is a splendid evergreen tree, rising, in its native country, to sixty feet or more, but with us scarcely exceeding thirty or forty feet. The leaves grow from eight inches to one foot long, in form not unlike those of the common laurel; the flowers are white, of a large size, and emit a pleasant fragrance. The plant is not so hardy as some other species, and should therefore be planted in a warm situation.

HIGH SOULED.

Set thou the first example of true greatness,
And pity an infatuated people.
What is't to thee, that others do the wrong?
Thou art *thyself*, amidst the worst injustice,
That hatred can heap upon thy head.
Revenge thy wrongs with magnanimity;
Build up thy virtue higher than the clouds
That human passion girts the good man with,
And let perpetual sunshine rest upon it.
Forgive thy country, pity her, and save!

DAWES.

His years but young, but his experience old;
His head unmellow'd, but his judgment ripe;
And, in a word, (for far behind his worth
Come all the praises that I now bestow,)
He is complete in feature, and in mind,
With all good grace to grace a gentleman.

SHAKSPEARE.

He was not born to shame:
Upon his brow shame is ashamed to sit;
For 'tis a throne where honour may be crown'd
Sole monarch of the universal earth.

SHAKSPEARE.

AIZE, or INDIAN CORN. *Zea mays.* Class 21, MONŒCIA. Order: TRIANDRIA. The native country of this valuable grain remains still undetermined. It is usually attributed to America, where it was cultivated by the aborigines at the time of the discovery; but no botanist has hitherto found it growing wild in any part of the new continent; and most certainly it does not so exist in any portion of the territory of the United States. It is also certain that its culture did not attract notice in Europe, Asia, or the north of Africa, till after the voyage of Columbus.

PLENTY.

In the young merry time of spring,
  When clover 'gins to burst;
When blue-bells nod within the wood,
  And sweet May whitens first;
When merle and mavis sing their fill,
Green is the young corn on the hill.

But when the merry spring is past,
  And summer groweth bold,
And in the garden and the field
  A thousand flowers unfold;
Before a green leaf yet is sere,
The young corn shoots into the ear.

When on the breath of autumn breeze,
  From pastures dry and brown,
Goes floating, like an idle thought,
  The fair, white thistle-down;
O, then what joy to walk at will,
Upon the golden harvest-hill.

                       HOWITT.

 APLE. *Acer Campestre.* Class 8, OCTAN-DRIA. Order : MONOGYNIA. The common maple belongs to a genus containing many species, of which it seems to be the only undisputed native. The sugar-maple is cultivated in various parts of our country for economical purposes. Nearly the entire consumption of sugar in some of the inland states is derived from this useful tree.

RESERVE. RETIREMENT.

Go,—pierce yon murky alley, where
None ever breathed untainted air,
Where all in vain the glorious sun
Struggles to chase the smoke-wreaths dun :
Ascend yon broken, winding stair,
Enter that room, what meets thee there ?
Nay, shrink not with fastidious pride,
But take thy stand that couch beside ;
There, though disease, and want, and pain,
Their victim bind with triple chain,
There shalt thou see earth's noblest sight,
A spirit wing'd for heavenward flight.
There Peace, sweet Peace, has found her way.
And turn'd thick midnight into day.

Now, hie thee hence, and dream no more
Of hermit's cell, and frugal store ;
Of skull, of *maple-dish*, or glass
Which marks how swift the hours do pass ;
But ply in Duty's path thy feet,
'T is likeliest there sweet Peace thou 'lt meet ;
And, if a lowly heart be thine,
Be sure she 'll make that heart her shrine.

ANON.

ARVEL OF PERU. *Mirabilis.* Class **5,** PENTANDRIA. Order: MONOGYNIA. This plant is called mirabilis, and with some degree of reason, for it is a most admirable flower; it expands its richly dyed corollas at night, whence it has been named by the French, *belle-de-nuit.*

It is universally considered to be the emblem of timidity from its shunning the brilliant light of day, and only venturing to display its charms in the cool of the evening.

The mimosa, or sensitive plant, has been assigned as the symbol of chastity and prudery, but we think it may be more properly used as the sign of timidity; as it seems to fly from the hand that would touch it. At the least approach, the leaves shrink within themselves. The petiole then droops, and if the plant be low, it touches the earth. Even a cloud passing between it and the rays of the sun, is sufficient to change the situation of its leaves and the general aspect of the plant.

> Timidity, of all afraid,
> Her wreath of the mimosa braid.

TIMIDITY.

> Think on th' insulting scorn, the conscious pangs,
> The future miseries that await th' apostate;
> So shall *timidity* assist thy reason,
> And wisdom into virtue turn thy frailty.
>
> JOHNSON.

> 'Solitaire amante des nuits,
> Pourquoi ces timides alarmes,
> Quand ma muse au jour que tu fuis
> S'apprête à révéler les charmes?
>
> Si, par pudeur, aux indiscrets
> Tu caches ta fleur purpurine,
> En nous dérobant tes attraits,
> Permets du moins qu'on les dévine."

ARYGOLD. *Calendula.* Class 19, SYN-
GENESIA. Order: POLYGAMIA NECESSARIA.
Madame Lebrun, in one of her charming
pictures, has represented grief as a young
man pale and languishing; his head appears
to be bowed down by the weight of a garland of marygolds. All the world knows
this gilded flower, which has been made the emblem of distress
of mind; or rather, we should say of that inquietude which is
caused by uncertainty as to the sentiments of the *one* we love
with a peculiar affection. The lover longs to know whether
there be a reciprocal feeling in the heart of his mistress towards
himself, or whether he has been buoying himself up with false
hope. We verily believe that there are few who would not prefer to receive the dread intelligence that his suit is rejected, than
remain in this uncertain state.

INQUIETUDE.

But be not long, for in the tedious minutes,
Exquisite interval, I'm on the rack;
For sure the greatest evil man can know,
Bears no proportion to the dread suspense.

FROWDE.

Uncertainty!
Fell demon of our fears! The human soul,
That can support despair, supports not thee.

MALLET.

Our doubts are traitors,
And make us lose the good we oft might win,
By fearing to attempt.

SHAKSPEARE.

Like a man to double business bound,
I stand in pause where I shall first begin,
And both neglect.

SHAKSPEARE.

EADOW SWEET. *Spiræa Ulmaria.* Class 12, ICOSANDRIA. Order: PENTAGYNIA. This plant, called by the French " *Reine des prés,*" is deemed an useless herb, because herbalists have not discovered any medical properties in it; and, also, because animals reject it as food. It is, however, a highly ornamental flower, and surely that ought to be accounted something.

USELESSNESS.

From worldly cares himself he did esloin,
And greatly shunned manly exercise;
From every work he challenged essoin,
For contemplation sake: yet otherwise,
His life he led in lawless riotise
By which he grew to grievous malady;
For in his lustless limbs through evil guise,
A shaking fever reign'd continually;
Such one was *Idleness.*

SPENSER.

Who doth to sloth his younger days engage,
For fond delight, he clips the wings of fame;
For sloth, the canker-worm of honour's badge,
Fame's feather'd wings doth fret; burying the name
Of virtue's worth in dust of dunghill shame,
Whom action out of dust to light doth bring,
And makes her mount to heav'n with golden wing.

ANON.

What is a man,
If his chief good and market of his time
Be but to sleep and feed? a beast, no more.
Sure, he that made us with such large discourse,
Looking before and after, gave us not
That capability and god-like reason
To rust in us unused.

SHAKSPEARE.

EZEREON. *Daphne Mezereon.* Class 8, OCTANDRIA. Order: MONOGYNIA. The stem of this plant is covered with a dry bark, which gives it the appearance of dead wood. To hide this, nature has surrounded each of its branches with a garland of purple flowers, which, unrolled in spiral form, and tipped with a small tuft of leaves, seems to assume the form of a pine-apple.

This fragrant and much-admired shrubbery plant frequently flourishes towards the end of January, appearing as it were in the breast of snows, reclad in its charming attire. It is regarded as the emblem of an imprudent and coquettish nymph, who, in the midst of winter, arrays herself in the robes of spring.

DESIRE TO PLEASE.

Mezereon too,
Though leafless, well attired, and thick beset
With blushing wreaths, investing every spray.
                                    COWPER.

Their in a kiss she breathed her various arts,
Of trifling prettily with wounded hearts;
A mind for love, but still a changing mind,
The lisp affected, and the glance design'd;
The sweet confusing blush, the secret wink,
The gentle swimming walk, the courteous sink,
The stare for strangeness fit, for scorn the frown;
For decent yielding, looks declining down,
The practised languish, where well-feign'd desire
Would own its melting in a mutual fire;
Gay smiles to comfort; April showers to move;
And all the nature, all the art of love.
                                    PARNELL.

IGNONETTE. *Reseda Odorata.* Class 11, DODECANDRIA. Order: TRIGYNIA. The odour exhaled by this little flower is thought by some to be too powerful for the house; but even those persons, we presume, must be delighted with the fragrance which it throws from the balconies into the streets of the city, giving something like a breath of garden air to the ' close-pent man,' whose avocations will not permit a ramble beyond the squares of the fashionable part of the town.

YOUR QUALITIES SURPASS YOUR CHARMS.

Now look ye on the plain and modest guise
Of yon unlovely flower — *unlovely?* — no —
Not *beautiful,* 't is true — not touch'd with hues
Like her's we late have gazed on; but so rich
In precious fragrance is that lovely one,
So loved for her sweet qualities, that I
Should woo her first amid a world of flowers;
For she is like some few beloved ones here,
Whom *eyes,* perchance, might slightingly pass o'er,
But whose true wisdom, gentleness, and worth,
Unchanging friendship, ever-faithful love,
And countless minor beauties of the mind,
Attach our *hearts* in deep affection still.

TWAMLEY.

No gorgeous flowers the meek reseda grace,
Yet sip with eager trunk yon busy race
Her simple cup, nor heed the dazzling gem
That beams in Fritillaria's diadem.

EVANS.

ISLETOE. *Viscum Alba.* Class 22, DIŒ-CIA. Order: TETRANDRIA. This plant, especially when found growing on the oak, was held in the greatest veneration by the Druids, which, having no attachment to earth, they considered to be of celestial origin. The utmost solemnity was used in the gathering of it; it took place always at the close of the year, when the moon was just six days old. Two white bulls, which had never felt the yoke, were fastened by their horns to the fortunate oak whereon the misletoe had been discovered; a priest, clad in a white vesture, then ascended the tree, and detached the plant with a golden hook or bill, whilst others stood ready to receive it in a white woollen cloth: this done, they then prepared to offer the best of their flocks and herds in sacrifice, " mumbling many orisons, and praying devoutly that it would please God to bless this gift of his to the good and benefit of all those to whom he had vouchsafed to give it." Water, in which it had been steeped, they considered a panacea for diseases of every description; hence the name they gave it, " omnia sanans," or " all-heal."

PARASITE.

" A parasite! I would not be,
    For worlds, that servile thing;
Not royalty itself, from me
E'er homage won of heart or knee;
    To Power I would not cling
(Like this vile plant to oaken bough),
Though it had kingdoms to bestow!"

'T is proudly said — yet pause — for Power
    A crown not always wears;
Oft hundred-headed (as of yore
The monster, famed in classic lore,)
    Its Proteus-form appears:
And thus disguised from mortal ken
Hast thou ne'er worshipp'd in its train?   ANON.

OTHERWORT. *Leonurus.* Class 14, DI-DYNAMIA. Order: GYMNOSPERMIA. The clandestina grows at the foot of large trees, in moist and umbrageous places. Its pretty purple flowers are nearly always hidden under moss or dry leaves: hence the propriety of the sentiment.

CONCEALED LOVE.

The secret by her tongue conceal'd,
  Her fading charms declare,
And what by words is unreveal'd,
  Is better written there;
The silent tale by sorrow traced,
Of 'young affections run to waste.'

The radiance of her downcast eye
  Is shadow'd by a tear,
Faint as the light of evening's sky,
  That tells the night is near; —
The long, the moonless night of rest,
  When life is waning in its west.

And seems her cheek, whose bloom is fled
  (So beautiful and brief),
As if the white rose there had shed
  Its frail and fallen leaf;
Which summer's genial sun and rain
Shall never wake to life again.

But she is hastening to the bowers
  That bloom in happier spheres;
Where fond affection's fadeless flowers
  Shall not be nurst by tears;
Where love's pure flame shall ne'er expire,
Nor kill the heart that feeds its fire.
                     ANON.

OUNTAIN ASH, or ROWAN TREE. *Pyrus Aucuparia*. Class 12, ICOSANDRIA. Order: PENTAGYNIA. The common appellation of this beautiful tree, the character of its foliage, and its choice of situation, have led to some confusion respecting its classification. Gerarde and Gilpin, for instance, have considered it a variety of the true ash (Fraxinus); an error which has not escaped the animadversions of later botanists, who all now concur in comprehending it in the genus Pyrus.

TALISMAN.

One effort more, and now I seem to stand
  On proud Helvellyn, — feel around me blow
The keen, fresh breeze; or tread "the silver strand"
  Of the blue lake, and watch its gentle flow:
Now pierce the glen where Ayrey's torrent boils,
  And mark the sunbeams dally with the spray,
Till o'er the troubled flood an Iris smiles,
  As if to charm its wrathful mood away;
Or pitying view each little flower, bright-hued,
Weeping its life away in sunless solitude.

Now glancing upward to a dizzy height,
  I see the *rowan* fling its feathery sprays
O'er the cleft rocks, with scarlet fruit so bright,
  It seems a sylvan Iris to my gaze.
Fairest of trees that love the rushing stream,
  The rocky glen, or mountain's shaggy side!
Ah! well, methinks, of yore might Fancy deem
  No evil thing could in thy presence bide;
So pure thou look'st, so fearless, and so free,
Owning nc spells thyself save beauty's witchery.

ANON.

OUSE-EAR, SCORPION-GRASS. *Myo-sotis Palustris*. Class 5, PENTANDRIA. Order: MONOGYNIA. This plant, so celebrated in German love-song, under the emblem of " *Vergisz mich nicht*," has hence been made to signify " forget me not," by all the son net writers of Europe.

> " Where time, on sorrow's page of gloom
>   Has fix'd its envious lot,
> Or swept the record from the tomb,
>   It says — Forget-me-not."

FORGET ME NOT.

The blue-eyed *Forget-me-Not*, beautiful flower,
Half-woo'd and half-stolen, I brought from her bower,
By the bright river's brink, where she nestled so low,
That the water o'er stem and o'er leaflet might flow;
As if, like Narcissus, she foolishly tried
To gaze on her own gentle face in the tide.

Half inclined, half reluctant, the flower bade adieu
To the friends left behind in the dell where she grew;
And a few shining drops, from the river-spray flung,
Like tears of regret on her azure eyes hung;
But I kiss'd them away, as a lover had done,
In joy that my fair river-beauty I'd won.

TWAMLEY.

Remember thee ?
Yea, from the table of my memory
I'll wipe away all trivial fond records,
All saws of books, all forms, all pressures past,
That youth and observation copied there;
And thy commandment all alone shall live
Within the book and volume of my brain,
Unmix'd with baser matter.

SHAKSPEARE.

YRTLE. *Myrtus.* Class 12, ICOSANDRIA. Order: MONOGYNIA. The oak has ever been consecrated to Jupiter,—the laurel to Apollo,—the olive to Minerva,—and the myrtle to Venus. Among the ancients the myrtle was a great favourite, for its elegance, and its sweet and glossy evergreen foliage. Its perfumed and delicate flowers seem destined to adorn the fair forehead of love, and are said to have been made the emblem of love, and dedicated to beauty, when Venus first sprang from the sea. We are informed by mythological writers that when the fair goddess first appeared upon the waves, she was preceded by the houris with a scarf of a thousand colours, and a garland of myrtle.

LOVE.

See, rooted in the earth, her kindly bed,
The unendanger'd myrtle, deck'd with flowers,
Before the threshold stands to welcome us!
WORDSWORTH.

Fall, rosy garlands, from my head!
Ye myrtle wreaths, your fragrance shed
Around a younger brow!
WORDSWORTH.

In peace, love tunes the shepherd's reed;
In war, he mounts the warrior's steed;
In halls, in gay attire is seen;
In hamlets, dances on the green;
Love rules the court, the camp, the grove,
And men below, and saints above;
For love is heaven, and heaven is love.
SCOTT.

Love the sense of right and wrong confounds,
Strong love and proud ambition have no bounds.
DRYDEN.

ARCISSUS, FALSE. *Narcissus Pseudo.* Class 6, HEXANDRIA. Order: MONOGYNIA. The flowers of this plant very often fail. It is a native of our meadows, but is cultivated with great care in Holland, and exported thence under the name of Phœnix, or Soleil d'or. After tending the forced plant with much care, we are surprised to find that we possess in it nothing better than the false narcissus.

DELUSIVE HOPE.

As rising on its purple wing
The insect queen of eastern spring,
O'er emerald meadows of Kashmere,
Invites the young pursuer near,
And leads him on from flower to flower,
A weary chase and wasted hour,
Then leaves him, as it soars on high,
With panting heart and tearful eye:
So beauty lures the full-grown child,
With hue as bright and wing as wild;
A chase of idle hopes and fears,
Begun in folly, closed in tears.

BYRON.

On life's gay stage, one inch above the grave,
The proud run up and down in quest of eyes;
The sensual, in pursuit of something worse;
The grave, of gold; the politic, of power;
And all, of other butterflies, as vain.

YOUNG.

How must a spirit, late escaped from earth,
The truth of things new blazing in its eye,
Look back, astonish'd, on the ways of men,
Whose lives' whole drift is to forget their graves!

YOUNG.

ARCISSUS. *Narcissus Poeticus.* Class 6, HEXANDRIA. Order: MONOGYNIA. The poet's narcissus exhales a very agreeable perfume; it bears a golden crown in the centre of its pure white petals, which expand quite flat, the stem slightly inclining to one side. The cup or nectary in the centre, which is very short, is frequently bordered with a bright purple circle, and sometimes the nectary is edged with crimson.

Ovid, in his Metamorphoses, tells us of the fate of the lovely and coy Narcissus. A thousand nymphs loved the handsome youth, but suffered the pains of unrequited love. Viewing himself in the crystal fount, he became enamoured of his own image.

EGOTISM.

How beautiful art thou, my winter Flower!
Lifting with graceful pride thy stately head,
Heavy with its rich crown of pearl and gold: —
Thou sheddest on the air such soft perfume,
That I could deem 't was incense, gently flung
Before thy beauty's shrine by some fair sprite
Enamour'd of thy maiden loveliness.
The hyacinth and violet entwined
Have scarce so sweet an odour.

      Thanks, my Flower,
My gentle, kind companion — for to me
Thy silence is most eloquent: — I love
Thy quiet steadfast gaze, as, o'er my desk,
The long day through thou hast seem'd watching me,
And ever and anon, in glancing up,
I still have met thy calm unchanging look
Reminding me, in silence, of the friend
Whose gift thou wert to me.
       TWAMLEY.

IGHT BLOOMING CEREUS. *Cactus Grandiflorus.* Class 12, ICOSANDRIA. Order: MONOGYNIA. The night-flowering Cereus, or *Cactus grandiflorus*, is one of our most splendid hot-house plants, and is a native of Jamaica and some other of the West India Islands. Its stem is creeping, and thickly set with spines. The flower is white, and very large, sometimes nearly a foot in diameter. The most remarkable circumstance with regard to the flower, is the short time which it takes to expand, and the rapidity with which it decays. It begins to open late in the evening, flourishes for an hour or two, then begins to droop, and before morning is completely dead.

TRANSIENT BEAUTY.

Now departs day's garish light —
  Beauteous flower, lift thy head !
Rise upon the brow of night !
  Haste, thy transient lustre shed !

Night has dropp'd her dusky veil —
  All vain thoughts be distant far,
While, with silent awe, we hail
  Flora's radiant evening star.

See to life her beauties start ;
  Hail ! thou glorious, matchless flower !
Much thou sayest to the heart,
  In the solemn, fleeting hour.

Ere we have our homage paid,
  Thou wilt bow thine head and die ;
Thus our sweetest pleasures fade,
  Thus our brightest blessings fly.

Sorrow's rugged stem, like thine,
  Bears a flower thus purely bright ;
Thus, when sunny hours decline,
  Friendship sheds her cheering light. ANON.

AK. *Quercus.* Class 5, PENTANDRIA. Order: POLYANDRIA. The ancients believed that the oak, created with the earth, offered food and shelter to the first parents of our kind. This tree is said to have shaded the cradle of Jupiter, to whom it was consecrated, after his birth, upon Mount Lycæus, in Arcadia. The oaken crown was less esteemed by the Greeks than the crown of gold ; but the Romans considered it the most desirable of all rewards.

HOSPITALITY

Proud monarch of the forest !
　That once, a sapling bough,
Didst quail far more at evening's breath
　Than at the tempest now,
Strange scenes have pass'd, long ages roll'd
　Since first upon thy stem,
Then weak as osier twig, Spring set
　Her leafy diadem.

To thee but little recks it
　What seasons come or go,
Thou lovest to breathe the gale of spring
　And bask in summer's glow,
But more to feel the wintry winds
　Sweep by in awful mirth,
For well thou know'st each blast will fix
　Thy roots more deep in earth.

Would that to me life's changes
　Did thus with blessings come !
That mercies might, like gale of spring,
　Cause some new grace to bloom !
And that the storm which scattereth
　Each earth-born hope abroad,
Might anchor those of holier birth
　More firmly on my God !　ANON.

LIVE. *Olea.* Class 2, DIANDRIA. Order: MONOGYNIA. This tree has been celebrated in all ages as the bounteous gift of heaven, and as the emblem of peace and plenty. Peace—wisdom—concord—clemency—joy —and the graces have ever been crowned with olive.

The dove sent out of the ark by Noah to ascertain if the waters were assuaged, returned bearing a branch of olive as a symbol of that rest which heaven was about to restore to the earth.

PEACE.

Sweet Teviot! on thy silver tide
  The glaring bale-fires blaze no more ;
No longer steel-clad warriors ride
  Along thy wild and willow'd shore ;
Where'er thou wind'st by dale or hill
All, all is peaceful, all is still,
  As if thy waves, since Time was born,
Since first they roll'd upon the Tweed,
Had only heard the Shepherd's reed,
    Nor started at the bugle-horn.

SCOTT.

    To thee the heavens, in thy nativity,
Adjudged an olive branch, and laurel crown,
As likely to be blest in peace and war.

SHAKSPEARE.

    Now no more the drum
Provokes to arms, or trumpet's clangour shrill
Affrights the wives, or chills the virgin's blood ;
But joy and pleasure open to the view
Uninterrupted !

PHILIPS.

In peace there 's nothing so becomes a man,
As modest stillness and humility.

SHAKSPEARE.

RANGE-TREE. *Citrus Aurantium.* Class 18, POLYADELPHIA. Order: ICOSANDRIA. This is a very ancient genus, and combines many excellencies in its species; it is a handsome evergreen; it has most odoriferous flowers, and brilliant, fragrant, and delicious fruits. Loudon observes, that "it is one of the most striking of fruit-bearing trees, and must have attracted the notice of aboriginal man long before other fruits of less brilliancy, but of more nutriment or flavour. The golden apples of the heathens, and forbidden fruit of the Jews, are supposed to allude to this family, though it is remarkable that we have no authentic records of any species of citrus having been known; certainly none were cultivated by the Romans." In the latter part of the seventeenth century it was a very fashionable tree in conservatories, where few exotics of other sorts were at that time to be found. It has been likened to a generous friend, who is ever loading us with favours.

GENEROSITY.

Ah, sweet cousin Blanche, let's see
What's the flower resembling thee!
With those dove-like eyes of thine,
And thy fair hair's silken twine;
With thy low, broad forehead, white
As marble, and as purely bright;
With thy mouth so calm and sweet,
And thy dainty hands and feet;
What's the flower most like thee?
Blossom of the *orange-tree!*

HOWITT.

O, my good lord, the world is but a word;
Were it all yours, to give it in a breath,
How quickly were it gone!

SHAKSPEARE.

ALM. *Palma.* Class 21, Monœcia. Order: Hexandria. Whatever praise may be awarded to the bay, there are few but will be disposed to give yet higher honour to the palm. Like its classic associate (with which it was often blended), it was considered an appropriate meed for the victor, but more generally it was reserved for religious triumphs; and from this, as well as from the prominent place it occupies in Holy Writ, we feel the epithet of " celestial palm," bestowed on it by Pope, not inapplicable.

VICTORY.

But there is a fame shall last,
When earth's flitting glory's past,
And a branch no adverse blast
    Shall destroy.

'T is, like bay, the victor's meed;
    But it decks not poet's grave,
Nor the warrior's martial deed,
    No—'t is only seen to wave
Where the martyr's honour'd dust doth repose,
    Or his, who broke the gloom
Long of pagan lands the doom,
And made " the desert bloom
    As the rose."

But where's the power of thought
    Which may pierce those scenes sublime,
When the Christian's fight is fought,
    And o'er Sin, and Death, and Time,
Through heaven-imparted might, he hath won
    When he joins the glorious band
Who as crowned victors stand,
With palm-branch in his hand,
    Round the throne?

                          Anon.

ASSION FLOWER. *Passiflora*. Class 5, PENTANDRIA. Order: TRIGYNIA. The *Murucuia* of the western world was no sooner seen in Italy, than fanciful devotion found a mysterious representation of the passion of Christ in this flower, and it received the sanctimonious titles of *Flos Passionis* and *Christi Passionis Imago*, from which our name of passion flower is derived, and the emblem formed.

PASSIONATE LOVE. RELIGIOUS SUPERSTITION.

Well art thou named — thou warm-hued Passion Flower,
Fit emblem of the ardour and caprice
Of that wild passion, Love : — for thou dost change,
Even like him, thy semblance; and thou art coy,
Ay, as the fairest maiden whose young heart
Thy namesake hath invaded. Coy, and proud,
For thou, forsooth, must have the bright sun come,
And wait, and gaze upon thy sleeping face,
Before thou wilt vouchsafe to ope thine eyes
Of starry beauty to our wondering gaze.
And then, ere long, the jealous petals close,
And shut within their selfish clasp the gem
They darken, not admire. And are there not
Some other selfish things in this strange world,
That do the like with flowers of lovelier growth ?
                                            TWAMLEY.

At rosy morn, or evening's silent hour,
Some fair enthusiast views the sainted flower,
When lo! to rapt imagination's eye,
Springs the sad scene of darken'd Calvary !
The thorny crown the heavenly brows around,
The scourging thorns, the galling cords that bound,
And nails that pierced with agonizing wound.
                                            SHAW.

ERIWINKLE, BLUE. *Vinca Minor.* Class 5, PENTANDRIA. Order: MONOGYNIA. There is an agreeable softness in the delicate blue colour of the periwinkle, and a quietness in the general aspect of the flower, that appears to harmonize with the retired situations where it loves to grow. It prefers the shady banks of the grove rather than to meet the meridian sun in the society of the gay plants of the parterre.

In France the flower has been made emblematical of the pleasures of memory, from the circumstance of Rousseau's saying, in one of his works, that as he and Madame Warens were proceeding to Charmettes, she was struck by the appearance of some blue flowers in the hedge, and exclaimed, "Here is the periwinkle still in flower." He then tells us, that thirty years afterwards, being at Gressier, with M. Peyron, climbing a hill, he observed some in blossom among the bushes, which bore his memory back at once to the time when he was walking with Madame Warens, and he inadvertently cried, "Ah! there is the periwinkle." Rousseau relates this anecdote as a proof of the vivid recollection he had of every incident which occurred at a particular time of his life, and hence this flower is made to represent "*Les doux Souvenirs.*"

SWEET REMEMBRANCES.

Though fate upon this faded flower
   His withering hand has laid,
Its odour'd breath defies his power,
   Its sweets are undecay'd.

And thus, although thy warbled strains
   No longer wildly thrill,
The memory of the song remains,
   Its soul is with me still.

DRAKE.

ERSICARIA. *Polygonum Oriental.* Class 8, OCTANDRIA. Order: DIGYNIA. The seeds of this Asiatic plant were procured by M. Tournefort, from the garden of the three Churches near Mount Ararat, the spot on which the ark is supposed to have rested, from whence it is selected for the emblem of restoration.

> Behold the different climes agree,
> Rejoicing in thy restoration.　　DRYDEN.

RESTORATION.

Yet it is not that age on my years has descended —
　'T is not that its snow-wreaths encircled my brow;
But the *newness* and sweetness of Being are ended —
　I feel not their love-kindling witchery now:
The shadows of death o'er my path have been sweeping —
　There are those who have loved me, debarr'd from the day,
The green turf is bright where in peace they are sleeping,
　And on wings of remembrance my soul is away.

It is shut to the glow of this present existence —
　It hears, from the Past, a funereal strain;
And it eagerly turns to the high-seeming distance,
　Where the last blooms of earth will be garner'd again;
Where no mildew the soft damask-rose cheek shall nourish
　Where Grief bears no longer the poisonous sting;
Where pitiless Death no dark sceptre can flourish,
　Or stain with his blight the luxuriant spring.

It is thus, that the hopes, which to others are given,
　Fall cold on my heart in this rich month of May;
I hear the clear anthems which ring through the heaven —
　I drink the bland airs that enliven the day;
And if gentle Nature, her festival keeping,
　Delights not my bosom, ah! do not condemn;
O'er the lost and the lovely my spirit is weeping,
　For the heart's fondest raptures are buried with them.
　　　　　　　　　　　　　　　　CLARK.

ERSIMON. *Diospyrus Virginiana.* Class 23, POLYGAMIA. Order: DIŒCIA. The Persimon, of the same genus as the Ebony, is a middling-sized tree, common in all parts of the United States south of lat. 41°. The fruit which is as large as a Plum, is very sweet when touched by the frosts, and frequently makes its appearance in our markets. An agreeable beverage is also obtained from it in some districts, by fermentation. The wood is used at Baltimore by turners, for large screws, and by tin-workers, for mallets; and at Philadelphia, for shoe-lasts; but though a common tree, it is usually of inconsiderable dimensions.

BURY ME AMID NATURE'S BEAUTIES.

In the wild forest-shade,
Under some spreading oak, or waving pine,
Or old elm, festoon'd with the gadding vine,
Let me be laid.

In this dim, lonely grot,
No foot, intrusive, will disturb my dust;
But o'er me songs of the wild bird shall burst —
Cheering the spot.

Not amidst charnel stones,
Or coffins dark, and thick with ancient mould —
With tatter'd pall, and fringe of canker'd gold,
May rest my bones.

But let the dewy rose,
The snow-drop, and the violet, lend perfume
Above the spot, where, in my grassy tomb,
I take repose.

Birds from the distant sea,
Shall sometimes hither flock on snowy wings,
And soar above my dust in airy rings,
Singing a dirge to me!   ANON.

IMPERNEL. *Anagallis Arvensis.* Class 5, PENTANDRIA. Order: MONOGYNIA. The common pimpernel is a beautiful trailing weed, and one of the *Floræ Horologicæ*, opening its flowers regularly about eight minutes past seven o'clock, and closing them about three minutes past two o'clock. It serves, also, as an hygrometer; for, if rain fall, or there be much moisture in the atmosphere, the flowers either do not open, or close up again. It is frequently called the shepherd's weather-glass.

ASSIGNATION.

Closed is the pink-eyed pimperne.,
. . . .
'Twill surely rain, I see, with sorrow,
Our jaunt must be put off to-morrow.

JENNER.

" I 'll go and peep at the Pimpernel,
  And see if she think the clouds look well;
      For if the sun shine,
      And 't is like to be fine,
      I shall go to the fair,
      For my sweetheart is there:
So, Pimpernel, what bode the clouds and the sky?
If fair weather, no maiden so merry as I."

Now the Pimpernel-flower had folded up
Her little gold star in her coral cup,
      And unto the maid
      Thus her warning said:
      " Though the sun smile down,
      There 's a gathering frown
O'er the chequer'd blue of the clouded sky;
So tarry at home, for a storm is nigh."

TWAMLEY.

INE APPLE. *Bromelia Ananas.* Class 6, HEXANDRIA. Order: MONOGYNIA. The fruit of the pine apple, surrounded by its beautiful leaves, and surmounted by a crown in which the germ of a plant is concealed, seems as though it were sculptured in massy gold. It is so beautiful that it appears to be made to please the eyes; so delicious that it unites the various flavours of our best fruits; and so odoriferous that we should cultivate it if it were only for its perfume.

YOU ARE PERFECT.

Never till now — never till now, O queen
    And wonder of the enchanted world of sound!
Never till now was such bright creature seen,
    Startling to transport all the regions round! —
Whence comest thou—with those eyes and that fine mien,
    Thou sweet, sweet singer? Like an angel found
Mourning alone, thou seem'st (thy mates all fled),
A star 'mongst clouds, — a spirit 'midst the dead!

Melodious thoughts hang round thee: — Sorrow sings
    Perpetual sweetness near, — divine despair!
Thou speak'st, — and music, with her thousand strings,
    Gives golden answers from the haunted air!
Thou movest, — and 'round thee Grace her beauty flings!
    Thou look'st, — and Love is born! Oh! songstress rare,
Lives there on earth a power like that which lies
In those resistless tones, — in those dark eyes?—

Oh, I have lived — how long! — with one deep treasure —
    One fountain of delight unlock'd, unknown;
But thou, the prophetess of my new pleasure,
    Hast come at last, and struck my heart of stone:
And now outgushes without stint or measure
    The endless rapture, — and in places lone
I shout it to the stars and winds that flee;
    And then I think on all I owe to thee!

                        CORNWALL.

INK. *Dianthus.* Class 10, DECANDRIA. Order: DIGYNIA. Cultivation has doubled the petals of this favourite flower, and procured for it an infinite variety of colouring, so that it is painted with a thousand shades, from the delicate rose-colour to the perfect white; and from a deep red to a brilliant scarlet. In some varieties we observe opposite colours placed together on the same flower; the pure white is tipped with crimson, and the rose-coloured is streaked with lively and brilliant red. We also see these beautiful flowers marbled, speckled, and at other times bisected in such manner that the deceived eye leads us to imagine that the same cup contains a purple flower, and one of palest alabaster.

LIVELY AND PURE AFFECTION.

Each pink sends forth its choicest sweet,
Aurora's warm embrace to meet.
ROBINSON.

True love's the gift which God has given
To man alone beneath the heaven.
. . . .
It is the secret sympathy,
The silver cord, the silken tie,
Which heart to heart, and mind to mind,
In body and in soul can bind.
SCOTT.

Now, Ladye — when a Cavalier
    Presents a chequer'd *Pink*,
'T is time to ascertain, my dear,
    His rent-roll you may think;
And then — provided his estate
    Don't meet your approbation,
It cannot, surely, be too late
    To cut — with a *Carnation.*
TWAMLEY.

LANE TREE. *Platanus.* Class 21, MONŒ-
CIA. Order: POLYANDRIA. The plane tree
has been appropriated as the symbol of genius, because the ancient Athenian philoso-
phers generally held their discourses, or retired to study under the agreeable shade of
its wide-spreading branches, for which it
was greatly esteemed at Athens. Xerxes is said to have been so
attracted by the charms of a plane tree, that he caused his army
of 1,700,000 men to halt, while he adorned the tree with all his
jewels, and with those of his concubines, and the principal lords
of his court, until the branches were loaded with ornaments of
every kind. He called it his mistress and his goddess; and it
was with difficulty that he was persuaded to leave the tree of
which he had become so extraordinarily enamoured.

GENIUS.

Not all unnoticed are thy forms of love,
   Peerless *America!* thy mountains rise
With cloudy coronals, and tower above
   The vegetable kingdom to the skies,
Calling upon thy sons to gaze with thee,
Starward in homage of the Deity.

Thy rivers swell majestic to the sea —
   In one eternal diapason, pour
Thy cataracts, the hymn of liberty,
   Teaching the clouds to thunder, — on thy shore
The Tritons dash their chariots, and tear
The adamantine echoes from their lair.

Where are thy bards, *America?* The lyre
   Hangs in its listless solitude too long;
Why should the song of nightingales expire,
   Because the rooks are screaming — raise their song
And still the dissonance their silence brings!
Bards of the mountain lyre, awake its strings!

DAWES

LUM TREE. *Prunus Domestica.* Class 12, ICOSANDRIA. Order: MONOGYNIA. Every year the plum tree is covered with an immense quantity of flowers, but unless trained and pruned by the hand of an able gardener of all its superfluous wood, it will only yield fruit once in three years.

KEEP YOUR PROMISES.

If this austere unsociable life
Change not your offer made in heat of blood;
If frosts, and fasts, hard lodging, and thin weeds,
Nip not the gaudy blossoms of your love,
But that it bear this trial, and last love;
Then, at the expiration of the year,
Come challenge me.

SHAKSPEARE.

Here is my hand for my true constancy;
And when that hour o'erslips me in the day,
Wherein I sigh not, Julia, for thy sake,
The next ensuing hour some foul mischance
Torment me, for my love's forgetfulness!

SHAKSPEARE.

His words are bonds, his oaths are oracles;
His love sincere, his thoughts immaculate;
His tears pure messengers sent from his heart;
His heart as far from fraud, as heaven and earth.

SHAKSPEARE.

God join'd my heart and Romeo's, thou our hands,
And ere this hand, by thee to Romeo seal'd,
Shall be the label to another deed,
Or my true heart with treacherous revolt
Turn to another, this shall slay them both.

SHAKSPEARE.

OPLAR, WHITE. *Populus Alba.* Class 22, Diœcia. Order: Octandria. The white poplar is one of the most valuable of trees, and grows to the height of more than ninety feet, towering its superb head upon a straight silvered trunk. The ancients consecrated it to time, because the leaves are in continual agitation; and being of a blackish green on the upper side, with a thick white cotton on the other; they were supposed to indicate the alternation of day and night.

TIME.

Yes, gentle time, thy gradual, healing hand
Hath stolen from sorrow's grasp the envenom'd dart;
Submitting to thy skill, my passive heart
Feels that no grief can thy soft power withstand;
And though my aching breast still heaves the sigh,
Though oft the tear swells silent in mine eye;
Yet the keen pang, the agony is gone;
Sorrow and I shall part; and these faint throes
Are but the remnant of severer woes.

Tighe.

"Where is the world," cries Young, "at eighty? Where
The world in which a man was born?" Alas!
Where is the world of eight years past? 'T was there—
I look for it—'t is gone, a globe of glass!
Crack'd, shiver'd, vanish'd, scarcely gazed on ere
A silent change dissolves the glittering mass.
Statesmen, chiefs, orators, queens, patriots, kings,
And dandies, all are gone on the wind's wings.

Byron.

The greatest schemes that human wit can forge,
Or bold ambition dares to put in practice,
Depend upon our husbanding a moment.

Rowe.

OPLAR, BLACK. *Populus Niger.* Class 22, Diœcia. Order: Octandria. This tree is consecrated to Hercules, who, according to the fable of the ancients, wore a crown made of its foliage when he descended into the infernal regions. This fable accounts for the different shades which the leaf has on either side in the following manner. The leaves on the side next the head of Hercules preserved their natural colour, or, some say, received that dim and pallid hue from the moisture on his brow; while those on the other side, being exposed to the smoke and vapour of the dismal regions he was visiting, were tinged with a darker shade, which they still retain.

COURAGE.

The poplar is by great Alcides worn.

VIRGIL.

The brave man seeks not popular applause,
Nor, overpower'd with arms, deserts his cause;
Unshamed, though foil'd, he does the best he can,
Force is of brutes, but honour is of man.

DRYDEN.

Whate'er betides, by destiny 't is done,
And better bear like men, than vainly seek to shun.

DRYDEN.

Be not dismay'd — fear nurses up a danger;
And resolution kills it in the birth.

PHILLIPS.

The human race are sons of sorrow born;
And each must have his portion. Vulgar minds
Refuse or cranch beneath their load: the brave
Bear theirs without repining.

MALLET

OPPY. *Papaver.* Class 13, POLYANDRIA. Order: MONOGYNIA. The poppy yields a narcotic juice in considerable quantity, which is frequently administered to procure sleep and relieve pain; on this account, it has been made the symbol of consolation. The ancients, who regarded sleep as the great physician, and the great consoler of human nature, crowned the god of sleep with a wreath of poppies.

CONSOLATION OF SLEEP.

Man's rich restorative; his balmy bath,
That supples, lubricates, and keeps in play
The various movements of this nice machine,
Which asks such frequent periods of repair.
When tired with vain rotations of the day,
Sleep winds us up for the succeeding dawn;
Fresh we spin on, till sickness clogs our wheels,
Or death quite breaks the spring, and motion ends.

                          YOUNG.

           Sleep's dewy wand
Has stroked my drooping lids, and promises
My long arrear of rest; the downy god
(Wont to return with our returning peace)
Will pay, ere long, and bless me with repose.

                          YOUNG.

The noon of night is past, and gentle sleep,
Which friendly waits upon the labour'd hind,
Flies from the embraces of a monarch's arms;
The mind disturb'd denies the body rest.

                          SLADE.

           Kind sleep affords
The only boon the wretched mind can feel;
A momentary respite from despair.

                          MURPHY.

RIMROSE. *Primula.* Class 5, PENTAN-
DRIA. Order: MONOGYNIA. The saffron
tufts of the primrose announce the return of
spring, when we see the snowy mantle of
retiring winter ornamented with embroidery
of verdure and of flowers. The season of
hoar frost has passed, but the bright days of
summer have not yet arrived. The period is emblematical of a
lovely girl just passing from childhood to youth.

EARLY YOUTH.

By the soft green light in the woody glade,
On the banks of moss where thy childhood play'd,
By the household tree through which ·thine eye
First look'd in love to the summer sky;
By the dewy gleam, by the very breath
Of the Primrose-tufts in the grass beneath,
Upon thy heart there is laid a spell,
Holy and precious — oh ! guard it well !

Yes ! when thy heart in its pride would stray
From the first pure loves of its youth away ;
When the sullying breath of the world would come
O'er the flowers it brought from its native home;
Think thou again of the woody glade,
Of the sound by the rustling Ivy made.
Think of the tree at thy father's door,
And the kindly spell shall have power once more.

TWAMLEY.

No smiling knot
Of early primroses, upon the warm,
Luxuriant, southern bank appears, unmark'd
By him.

CARRINGTON.

YRUS JAPONICA. *Pyrus Japonica.* Class 12, ICOSANDRIA. Order: TRIGYNIA. The brilliant colours and woody growth of the Pyrus Japonica make it contrast strikingly with the pale and fragile snow-drop, near whose modest bells this superb native of Japan may often be seen. The buds and flowers of brightest crimson, with their golden-coloured anthers, come peering out through the snow-wreaths that lie lightly upon their trained stems. The white and pink varieties of the Pyrus Japonica are also very beautiful, but have not the rich and glowing splendour of the crimson, which, from its hardiness, is more worthy of our esteem than most of our foreign acquisitions, that generally require the shelter of the green-house.

THE FAIRIES' FIRE.

Ha! are *they* out?
My summer friends, the fairies? Surely not;
Yet who but they have lit these tiny fires,
That gleam and glow amid the wintry scene?
Yes, here they are, aweary of the storms,
And wrecking winds, and pinching frosts, that keep
Within their darksome prison-house of earth
The gay and spendthrift flowers; here they are,
Lighting their ruddy beacons at the sun
To melt away the snow. See, how it falls
In drops of crystal from the glowing spray,
Wreathed with deep crimson buds — the fairy fires.
And now that there is something bright on earth,
The clouds are driven from the clear blue sky,
And heaven is bright'ning too. Serene and calm,
The very air is hushed into repose,
That not a breath may ruffle the young flowers,
Now gently waking into life and light.

TWAMLEY.

UAMOCLIT. *Ipomœa.* Class 5, PENTAN-
DRIA. Order: MONOGYNIA. The name
Quamoclit is an Indian one, used by the botanists Plumier and Tournefort as generic,
but by Linnæus only as a specific name of a
pretty species of Ipomœa, sometimes called
busybody. It is a native of the East Indies.

BUSYBODY.

O, he's as tedious
As is a tired horse, a railing wife;
Worse than a smoky house: — I had rather live
With cheese and garlic, in a windmill, far,
Than feed on cates, and have him talk to me,
In any summer-house in Christendom.

SHAKSPEARE.

This is a slight unmeritable man,
Meet to be sent on errands.
. . . .
And though we lay these honours on this man,
To ease ourselves of divers slanderous loads,
He shall but bear them as the ass bears gold,
To groan and sweat under the business,
Either led or driven, as we point the way;
And having brought our treasure where we will,
Then we take down his load, and turn him off,
Like to the empty ass, to shake his ears,
And graze in commons.

SHAKSPEARE.

A very superficial, ignorant, unweighing fellow.

SHAKSPEARE.

I am a feather for each wind that blows.

SHAKSPEARE.

AGGED ROBIN. *Lychnis.* *Flos Cuculi.* Class 10, DECANDRIA. Order: PENTAGYNIA. This flower is called Ragged Robin, on account of the finely-cut and ragged appearance of its petals. It is also called Cuckoo Flower, because it makes its appearance at the same time with that feathery harbinger of summer.

DANDY.

A man of taste is Robinet,
  A dandy, spruce and trim:
Whoe'er would dainty fashions set,
  Should go and look at him.

Rob scorns to wear his crimson coat
  As common people do,
He folds and fits it in and out,
  And does it bravely, too.

Oh! Robin loves to prank him rare
  With fringe, and flounce, and all;
Till you 'd take him for a lady fair,
  Just going to a ball.

Robin's a roguish, merry lad,
  He dances in the breeze,
And looks up with a greeting glad
  To the rustling hedge-row trees.

How civilly he beckons in
  The busy Mrs. Bee;
And she tells her store of gossiping
  O'er his honey and his glee.

All joy — all mirth — no carking care,
  No worldly woe has he;
Alack! I wish my lot it were,
  To live as happily!   TWAMLEY.

ANUNCULUS, ASIATIC. *Ranunculus Asiaticus.* Class 13, POLYANDRIA. Order: POLYGYNIA. The Asiatic ranunculus blooms amid our parterres in the earliest days of spring, spreading forth its varied lustrous flowers, which, shining with innumerable hues, are radiant with attractions. No other plant offers so rich a variety of colour to amateurs, "from a black down to white, through all the shades of reds, yellows, browns, and, indeed, excepting blue, every colour may be found in these gaily-painted flowers."

YOU ARE RADIANT WITH CHARMS.

Light as the angel-shapes that bless
An infant's dream, yet not the less
Rich in all woman's loveliness;—
With eyes so pure, that from their ray
Dark Vice would turn abash'd away,
Blinded, like serpents when they gaze
Upon the emerald's virgin blaze!—
Yet fill'd with all youth's sweet desires,
Mingling the meek and vestal fires
Of other worlds with all the bliss,
The fond, weak tenderness of this!
A soul, too, more than half divine,
  Where, through some shades of earthly feeling,
Religion's soften'd glories shine,
  Like light through summer foliage stealing,
Shedding a glow of such mild hue,
So warm, and yet so shadowy too,
As makes the very darkness there
More beautiful than light elsewhere!

MOORE.

ED BAY. *Laurus Carolinensis.* Class 9, ENNENDRIA. Order: MONOGYNIA. The Red Bay grows in the southern swamps, beyond lat. 37°, and attains the height of 60 or 70 feet, with the trunk 15 or 20 inches in diameter. The leaves resemble those of the Mediterranean species, and like them, may be employed in cookery. The wood is of a beautiful rose-colour, is strong, fine-grained, and acquires a brilliant polish. Before the introduction of mahogany, it was commonly employed in the southern states, and afforded highly beautiful articles of furniture. When of sufficient size, it is employed in ship-building, and exported for the purpose to New-York and Philadelphia.

LOVE'S MEMORY.

Oh, thou, who art the fairest of earth's daughters,
   Delighted could I sit a summer's day,
   To drink the music of thy lips away,
Gushing their careless melody as waters,
   And while I gazed upon thy full blue eyes,
Still listening to thy passion-kindling songs,
   Deem myself happiest of thy votaries.
Thus while the morning lark his notes prolongs,
   Lists the rapt bard, and bending to the skies,
Sends up the incense of a grateful heart,
   For such a gleam of heavenly ecstacies.
Oh, beautiful in feature, — as thou art
   More beautiful in mind, — my thoughts of thee
   Shall live in *Love's* undying *memory!*

DAWES.

We will revive those times, and in our memories
Preserve, and still keep fresh, like flowers in water,
Those happier days; when at our eyes our souls
Kindled their mutual fires, their equal beams
Shot and return'd, till, link'd and twined in one,
They chain'd our hearts together.

DENHAM.

RED MULBERRY. *Morus rubra.* Class 21, Monœcia. Order: Tetrandria. The Red Mulberry is rare in the Atlantic States, but abundant in the west, where it often exceeds 60 or 70 feet in height, with the trunk two feet in diameter. The fruit is deep red, of an agreeable, acidulous, and sugary flavour. The wood is fine-grained, compact, and by many is esteemed fully equal in durability to the locust; but the tree is less abundant, grows more slowly, and requires a richer soil. It is used in ship-building whenever it can be procured.

WISDOM.

O wisdom! if thy soft control
Can soothe the sickness of the soul,
Can bid the warring passions cease,
And breathe the calm of tender peace;
Wisdom! I bless thy gentle sway,
And ever, ever will obey.
But if thou comest with frown austere
To nurse the brood of care and fear;
To bid our sweetest passions die,
And leave us in their room a sigh;
Or if thine aspect stern have pow'r
To wither each poor transient flower
That cheers this pilgrimage of woe,
And dry the springs whence hope should flow;
Wisdom, thine empire I disclaim:
In gloomy shade of cloister dwell,
But never haunt my cheerful cell.

BARBAULD.

And that old mulberry that shades the court
Has been my joy from very childhood up.

WHITE.

OSE BUD. Who can say whether the white rose, or the red, the budding, or the full blown, has been most celebrated? Oft, indeed, have all been sung; and the rose bud, from its grace, and gradually maturing beauty, has not been inappropriately made emblematical of a young girl.

YOUNG GIRL.

The gentle budding rose, quoth she, behold,
That first scant peeping forth with morning beams,
Half ope, half shut, her beauties doth unfold,
In its fair leaves, and less seen, fairer seems;
And after spreads them forth, more fair and bold.

FAIRFAX.

A maid of sixteen years, of twilight eyes,
Deep set and dark, and fringed with pencil dyes,
Her forehead not too high, where thick black hair,
Comb'd smooth and parted, show'd the whiteness there;
Her lips of changeless carmine, often parted
With dimpling smiles, when sweet sensation started
In thoughts so pure, an angel's self would choose them,
Robed in the blush that mantled from her bosom;
Her form of rounded symmetry, where art
That makes so many beauties, bore no part;
With mind untutor'd, yet so constituted,
She never spake amiss, nor e'er disputed;
A girl like this, who would not love and cherish?
Or having won her heart, could leave that heart to perish?

DAWES.

The bloom of opening flowers' unsullied beauty,
Softness, and sweetest innocence she wears,
And looks like nature in the world's first spring.

ROWE.

OSE, HUNDRED-LEAVED. *Rosa Centifolia.* This is the rose with which painters choose to represent Love and Hymen; but, why it is selected from amongst the roses as the emblem of Grace we know not, since the regularity of its petals renders it less graceful than several other roses.

GRACE.

EMILIA.—Of all flowers,
Methinks a Rose is best.
SERVANT.—Why, gentle Madam?
EMILIA.—It is the very emblem of a maid:
For when the west wind courts her gently,
How modestly she blows, and paints the sun
With her chaste blushes! When the north comes near her,
Rude and impatient, then, like Chastity,
She locks her beauties in her bud again,
And leaves him to base briars.

BEAUMONT.

Fair ladies mask'd are roses in their bud:
Dismask'd, their damask sweet commixture shown,
Are angels veiling clouds, or roses blown.

SHAKSPEARE.

Her ivory-polish'd front with seemly cheer,
Graced at the bottom with a double bow,
Where all the Graces in their throne appear,
Where love and awful majesty do grow,
Expends itself, and shows a field more clear
Than candid lilies or the virgin snow;
Her eyes, like suns, shoot rays more sharp than darts,
Which wound all flinty love-despising hearts.

PORDAGE.

OSE BUD, WHITE.   Before the breath of love animated the world, all the roses were white, and every heart was insensible. Herrick says, that

> As Cupid danced among
> The Gods, he down the nectar flung;
> Which on the white rose being shed,
> Made it for ever after red.

Another poet makes the rose to say,

> 'T was from Love I borrow'd, too,
> My sweet perfume, my purple hue.

THE HEART THAT KNOWS NOT LOVE.

Thou, my love, art sweeter far than balmy
Incense in the purple smoke; pure and
Unspotted as the cleanly ermine, ere
The hunter sullies her with his pursuit;
Soft as her skin; chaste as th' Arabian bird
That wants a sex to woo, or as the dead,
That are divorced from warmth, from objects,
And from thought.

DAVENANT.

Oh! she is colder than the mountain's snow.
To such a subtle purity she's wrought,
She's pray'd and fasted to a walking thought:
She's an enchanted feast, most fair to sight,
And starves the appetite she does invite;
Flies from the touch of sense, and if you dare
To name but love, she vanishes to air.

CROWN.

In thy fair brow there's such a legend writ
Of chastity, as blinds the adulterous eye:
Not the mountain ice,
Congeal'd to crystals, is so frosty chaste,
As thy victorious soul, which conquers man,
And man's proud tyrant-passion.

DRYDEN.

OSE, WILD. The wild, or common dog-rose, has been made the emblem of simplicity. It forms one of the principal flowers in the rustic's bouquet.

> The wild rose scents the summer air,
> And woodbines weave in bowers,
> To glad the swain sojourning there,
> And maidens gathering flowers. CLARE.

Clemence Isaure, who instituted the floral games, awarded a single rose as the prize for eloquence.

The standards of the houses of York and Lancaster were charged with the bearing of the wild rose. This flower was also stamped on the current coin of those days.

> Thou once wast doomed
> Where civil discord braved the field,
> To grace the banner and the shield.
>
> ANON.

SIMPLICITY.

Ah yes, the poor man's garden!
  It is great joy to me,
This little, precious piece of ground
  Before his door to see!

The rich man has his gardeners,—
  His gardeners young and old;
He never takes a spade in hand,
  Nor worketh in the mould.

It is not with the poor man so,—
  Wealth, servants, he has none;
And all the work that's done for him
  Must by himself be done.

All day upon some weary task
  He toileth with good will;
And back he comes, at set of sun,
  His garden-plot to till.

HOWITT.

OSE, SWEET-BRIAR. *Rosa Suaveolens.* Class 12, ICOSANDRIA. Order: POLYGYNIA. This is the common Sweet-Briar of our country. The flowers and the leaves both shed a delicious fragrance. It is a great favourite with florists as well as poets and sentimental writers of all classes.

IMAGINATION.

Then Fancy beckon'd, and with smiling mien,
A radiant form arose, like the fair Queen
Of Beauty: from her eye divinely bright,
A richer lustre shot, a more attractive light.
She said, " With fairer tints I can adorn
The living landscape, fairer than the morn.
The summer-clouds in shapes romantic roll'd,
And those that edge the fading west, like gold;
The lake that sleeps in sun-light, yet impress'd
With shades more sweet than real, on its breast;
'Mid baffling stones, beneath a partial ray,
The small brook huddling its uneven way;
The bluey fading hills, the silvery sea,
And every scene of summer speaks of me:
But most I wake the sweetest wishes warm,
Where the fond gaze is turn'd on woman's breathing **form.'**

So passing silent through a myrtle grove,
Beauty first led him to the bower of Love.
A mellow light through the dim covert stray'd,
And opening roses canopied the shade.
Why does the hurrying pulse unbidden leap?
Behold, in yonder glade the Nymph asleep!
The heart-struck Minstrel hangs, with ling'ring gaze,
O'er every charm his eye impassion'd strays!

BOWLES.

OSE, YELLOW. *Rosa Lutea.* Ludovico Verthema tells us that, in the year 1503, he saw great quantities of yellow roses at Calicut, whence it is believed that both the single and double varieties were brought into Europe by the Turks, as Parkinson mentions that it was introduced into England by one Master Nicholas Lete, a worthy merchant of London, and a great lover of flowers, from Constantinople, which was first brought thither from Syria. It perished with Lete, but afterwards others were transmitted to Master John de Frangueville, also a merchant of London, and a great lover of all rare plants, as well as flowers, from whicharesprung the many varieties now flourishing in England.

It is well known that yellow is the colour of infidelity. The yellow rose also seems to appertain to the unfaithful in love or friendship. Water injures it; the sun scorches it; and this scentless flower, which profits neither by attention nor liberty, seems only to prosper when under restraint. When we wish to see them in their full brilliancy, it is necessary to incline the buds towards the earth, and keep them in that position by force.

INFIDELITY.

Take back the sigh, thy lips of art
In passion's moment breathed to me;
Yet, no — it must not, will not part,
'T is now the life-breath of my heart,
And has become too pure for thee!
Take back the kiss, that faithless sigh
With all the warmth of truth imprest;
Yet, no — the fatal kiss may lie,
Upon thy lips its sweets would die,
Or bloom to make a rival blest!
Take back the vows that, night and day,
My heart received, I thought, from thine;
Yet, no — allow them still to stay,
They might some other heart betray,
As sweetly as they've ruin'd mine!   MOORE.

OSE, WHITE. The god of silence was represented under the form of a young man, with one finger placed on his lips, and holding a white rose in the other hand. We are told that Love gave him this rose to secure his favour. The ancients sculptured a rose over the doors of their festive halls to interdict the guests from repeating anything that was spoken. Byron has rendered it sacred to the silence of the tomb. In the "Bride of Abydos" he says that, o'er the tomb of Zuleika

> A single rose is shedding
>   Its lovely lustre, meek and pale:
> It looks as planted by despair—
>   So white, so faint, the slightest gale
> Might whirl the leaves on high.

SILENCE.

> Still-born Silence, thou that art
> Floodgate of the deeper heart;
> Offspring of a heavenly kind;
> Frost o' th' mouth and thaw o' th' mind;
> Secrecy's confidant, and he
> That makes religion mystery;
> Admiration's speaking'st tongue —
> Leave thy desert shades, among
> Reverend hermits' hallow'd cells,
> Where retired'st devotion dwells;
> With thy enthusiasms come;
> Seize this maid, and make her dumb.
>
> FLECKNOE.

> You know my wishes ever yours did meet:
> If I be silent, 't is no more but fear
> That I should say too little when I speak.
>
> CAREW.

OSE. *Rosa.* Class 12, ICOSANDRIA. Order: POLYGYNIA. In producing this flower, nature appears to have exhausted herself by her prodigality, in attempting to create so fine a specimen of freshness, of beauty in form, of exquisite perfume, of brilliancy of colour, and of grace. The rose adorns the whole earth, as it is the commonest of flowers. The same day that its beauty is perfected it dies; but each spring restores it to us with renewed freshness. Poets have had fair opportunities for singing its praises, yet they have not rendered its eulogy common-place, but its name alone redeems *their* names from forgetfulness. Emblem of all ages,—interpreter of all our sentiments,—the rose mingles in the gaiety of our feasts, in our happiness, and in our sorrows. It is also the ornament of beauty, and lends its soft carnation hues to the blush of modesty. It is given as the prize of virtue; and is the image of youth, of innocence, and of pleasure. Venus is said to feel that she has a rival in the rose, as it possesses, like her, a grace which is more lovely than beauty itself.

BEAUTY.

A native grace
Sat fair proportion'd on her polish'd limbs,
Veil'd in a simple robe, their best attire,
Beyond the pomp of dress; for loveliness
Needs not the foreign aid of ornament,
But is, when unadorn'd, adorn'd the most;
Thoughtless of beauty, she was Beauty's self,
Recluse amid the close embowering woods.
As in the hollow breast of Apennine,
Beneath the shelter of encircling hills,
A myrtle rises far from human eye,
And breathes its balmy fragrance o'er the wild;
So flourish'd, blooming, and unseen by all,
The sweet Lavinia.

THOMSON.

OSE, MULTIFLORA. *Rosa Multiflora.* Class 12, ICOSANDRIA. Order: POLYGYNIA. A very beautiful variety of the rose, and justly a favourite among American florists. Its multitude of flowers renders it a suitable ornament for the portico or verandah of a country house, or the window of a boudoir.

MANY CHARMS.

I know a spot where poets fain would dwell,
  To gather flowers and food for afterthought,
As bees draw honey from the rose's cell,
  To live among the treasures they have wrought;
And there a cottage from a sylvan screen,
Sent up its curling smoke amidst the green.

Around that hermit-home of quietude,
  The elm-trees whisper'd with the summer air,
And nothing ever ventured to intrude,
  But happy birds that caroll'd wildly there,
Or honey-laden harvesters that flew
Humming away to drink the morning dew.

Around the door the honey-suckle climb'd,
  And *Multa-flora* spread her countless roses,
And never minstrel sang nor poet rhymed
  Romantic scene where happiness reposes,
Sweeter to sense than that enchanting dell,
Where home-sick memory fondly loves to dwell.
                    ANON.

The bloom of opening flowers' unsullied beauty,
Softness, and sweetest innocence she wears,
And looks like nature in the world's first spring.
                    ROWE.

OSE, MUSK.   This species of the rose lacks freshness.   Its mean flowers would be entirely without effect if they did not grow in panicles, containing from twenty to one hundred or more.   They please by their fine and musky odour, exhaled from their white blossoms in the autumnal months.   'T is said to be a native of Barbary, and is found wild in the hedges and thickets of the kingdom of Tunis.   This plant seems full of caprice.   It languishes suddenly in situations which at first appeared to be most favourable to its growth,—one year it displays innumerable bouquets, and the next it may not flower at all.

CAPRICIOUS BEAUTY

T is not the fairest form, that holds
    The mildest, purest soul within;
'T is not the richest plant that folds
    The sweetest breath of fragrance in;

And oft within the rose's bower,
    A lurking insect lies unknown,
That steals the honey from the flower,
    Before its outward grace has flown.

Then should a rude wind come at length,
    To break the quiet reigning round,
The flower that had the look of strength,
    Falls scarcely heeded to the ground.

Then, lady ! cast thy pride away,
    And chase those rebel thoughts of thine;
The casket may be bright and gay,
    Yet all within refuse to shine.

DAWES.

OSE, MOSS. The elegant moss rose is commonly supposed to be the offspring of the Provence rose, though some consider it to belong to the family of hundred-leaved roses. It has ever been made the emblem of perfected joy; Milton mentions it as " without thorn, the rose;" and an anonymous writer has sung of it in that character.

PLEASURE WITHOUT ALLOY.

Oh! I love the sweet blooming, the pretty moss rose,
  'T is the type of true pleasure, and perfected joy;
Oh! I envy each insect that dares to repose
  'Midst its leaves, or among its soft beauties to toy.

I love the sweet lily, so pure and so pale,
  With a bosom as fair as the new-fallen snows;
Her luxuriant odours she spreads through the vale,
  Yet e'en she must yield to my pretty moss rose.

Oh! I love the gay hearts-ease, and violet blue,
  The sun-flower and blue-bell, each flow'ret that blows,
The fir-tree, the pine-tree, acacia, and yew,
  Yet e'en these must yield to my pretty moss rose.

Yes, I love my moss rose, for it ne'er had a thorn,
  'T is the type of life's pleasures, unmix'd with its woes;
'T is more gay, and more bright, than the opening morn —·
  Yes, all things must yield to my pretty moss rose.

ANON.

Though duller thoughts succeed,
The bliss e'en of a moment, still is bliss.
Thou would'st not of her dew-drops spoil the thorn,
Because her glory will not last till noon;
Nor still the lightsome gambols of the colt,
Whose neck to-morrow's yoke will gall. Fye on't!
If this be wise, 't is cruel.

BAILLIE.

OSE, MONTHLY.   This plant, so frequently seen clustering round the cottage porch, as well in the immediate outskirts of busy smoky towns, as in the remotest vales, was originally brought to England in 1789.   It was then thought so delicate as to require the constant heat of the stove, and small cuttings were sold for several guineas each.   This was soon found not to be necessary ; and, in a short time, almost every country casement was ornamented by this Chinese beauty ; until the cottagers, wanting means to purchase flower-pots, planted them in the open ground ; where, persevering in the habits of a warmer climate, they quickly surpassed, in strength and beauty, all the inmates of the " gardens in which art supplies the fervour and the force of Indian skies."

This is the earliest flowering rose ; and, in mild seasons, when planted against a wall, will sometimes flower in the beginning of April ; and, being protected by glass in autumn, or aided by artificial heat, may be continued in bloom till Christmas.

BEAUTY EVER NEW.

Hurrah for the Prairie! no blight on *its* breeze,
No mist from the mountains, no shadow from trees,
It steals, incense-loaded, that gale, from the west,
As bees from the Prairie-rose fly to the nest.

Then fly to the Prairie, sweet maiden, with me,
The vine and the Prairie-rose cluster for thee,
And, hailing the moon in the prairie-propt sky,
The mocking-bird echoes the katy-did's cry.

There is nothing to cloy in the wilds of the West,
Each day has its pleasure, each evening its zest,
Our toil is a pastime, our rifles afford
The joy of the chase and the food for the board.

MITCHELL.

OSEMARY. *Rosemarinus.* Class 2, DIAN-DRIA. Order: MONOGYNIA. This shrub yields by distillation a light pale essential oil of great fragrance, which is imparted to rectified spirit. It was formerly recommended for strengthening the nervous system, headaches, &c., as well as to strengthen the memory. Rosemary has also been made the emblem of fidelity, and used accordingly, to be worn at weddings, and, on the same principle, at funerals. It is the principal ingredient in Hungary water, and is drank at tea for headaches, and by nervous persons.

YOUR PRESENCE REVIVES ME.

Rise from the dells where ye first were born,
From the tangled beds of the weed and thorn,
Rise, for the dews of the morn are bright,
And haste away, with your eyes of light.
—Should the green-house patricians, with withering frown,
On your simple vestments look haughtily down,
Shrink not, for His finger your heads hath bow'd
Who heeds the lowly, and humbles the proud.
—The tardy spring, and the chilling sky,
Hath meted your robes with a miser's eye,
And check'd the blush of your blossoms free;
With a gentler friend your home shall be;
To a kinder ear you may tell your tale
Of the zephyr's kiss, and the scented vale:
Ye are charmed! ye are charmed! and your fragrant sigh
Is health to the bosom on which ye die.

SIGOURNEY.

All nature fades extinct; and she alone
Heard, felt, and seen, possesses every thought,
Fills every sense, and pants in every vein.

THOMSON.

UE. *Ruta Graveolens.* Class 10, DECAN-
DRIA. Order: MONOGYNIA. This plant was
formerly called Herb of Grace, from its being used to sprinkle holy water.

> "Here did she drop a tear; here in this place
> I'll set a bank of rue, sour herb of grace."

GRACE, OR PURIFICATION.

———— Bow and sue for grace
With suppliant knee.
MILTON.

————Reverend sirs,
For you there's rosemary and rue; these keep
Seeming and savour all the winter long:
Grace and remembrance be to you both.
SHAKSPEARE.

O momentary grace of mortal man,
Which we more hunt for than the grace of God,
Who builds his hope in air of your fair looks,
Lives like a drunken sailor on a mast;
Ready, with every nod, to tumble down
Into the fatal bowels of the deep.
SHAKSPEARE.

'T is ever thus when favours are denied;
All had been granted but the thing we beg;
And still some great unlikely substitute,
Your life, your souls, your all of earthly good,
Is proffer'd in the room of one small boon.
BAILLIE.

No trifle is so small as what obtains,
Save that which loses favour; 't is a breath
Which hangs upon a smile! a look, a word,
A frown, the air-built tower of fortune shakes,
And down the unsubstantial fabric falls.
MORE.

CARLET IPOMŒA, or INDIAN JAS-
MINE. *Ipomœa Coccinea.* Class 5, PENT-
ANDRIA. Order: MONOGYNIA. This beautiful twining plant is a species of bindweed,
or something analogous; like the convolvulus, it requires something to support its
light tendrils; and, without fatiguing that
support, wreaths it with verdure and flowers.

I ATTACH MYSELF TO YOU.

Oh! let me only breathe the air,
  The blessed air that's breathed by ᴅhee;
And whether on its wings it bear
  Healing or death, 'tis sweet to me!
There, — drink my tears, while yet they fall —
  Would that my bosom's blood were balm,
And, — well thou knowest, — I'd shed it all
  To give thy brow one minute's calm.
Nay, turn not from me that dear face —
  Am I not thine — thy own loved bride —
The one, the chosen one, whose place
  In life or death is by thy side?
Think'st thou that she, whose only light,
  In this dim world, from thee hath shone,
Could bear the long, the cheerless night,
  That must be hers when thou art gone?
That I can live and let thee go,
Who art my life itself? — No, no,—
When the stem dies, the leaf that grew
Out of its heart must perish too!
Then turn to me, my own love, turn,
Before, like thee, I fade and burn;
Cling to these yet cool lips and share
The last pure life that lingers there!
                        MOORE.

COTCH FIR. *Pinus Sylvestris.* Class 21, Monœcia. Order: Monadelphia. The Scotch fir, taking all things into consideration, is esteemed the most valuable of the pines. It is the only one indigenous in the north and west of Europe, and grows abundantly in all the countries north of the Baltic, to the seventieth degree of latitude.

ELEVATION.

Thy throne a rock! thy canopy the skies!
And, circled in the mountain's dark embrace,
'Mid what stern pomp thy towering branches rise!
How wild, how lonely is thy dwelling-place!
In the rich mead a God of love we trace,
We feel His bounty in the sun and shower;
But here His milder glories shun our gaze,
Lost in the one dread attribute of power.
I cannot choose but wish thou hadst a fairer bower.

Yet to the scene thy stately form doth give
Appropriate grace; and in thy mountain-hold,
Like flowers with zephyrs "at the shut of eve,"
Thou with the storm hast dallied from of old.
But stateliness of form and bearing bold
Are not thy only boast: there dwells in thee
A soft, sweet spell (if we be rightly told),
Which waiteth but the touch of harmony,
To smooth the brow of care, and make e'en sorrow **flee.**

Anon.

He above the rest
In shape and gesture proudly eminent
Stood like a tower; his form had not yet lost
All her original brightness, nor appear'd
Less than archangel ruin'd.

Milton.

NOWDROP. *Galanthus.* Class 6, HEX-
ANDRIA. Order: MONOGYNIA. The north
wind whistles, and the hoar frost clothes the
verdure-despoiled trees; an uniform white
carpet covers the earth,—the birds withhold
their tuneful song,—and the sealed waters
cease to murmur as they roll along; the
rays of the sun, enfeebled by the density of our atmosphere, shed
a gloomy light over our fields; and the heart of man is sad, while
all nature reposes in torpid tranquillity.

Thus Madame de La Tour describes the state of nature, when
suddenly a delicate flower pierces through the veil of snow which
had concealed it. It has been aptly termed by her countrymen
Perce neige, from the quality just named; and is with equal
propriety called snow-drop in America.

CONSOLATION.

The rose is for the nightingale,
  The heather for the lark;
But the holly greets the red-breast
  'Mid winter drear and dark;
And the snow-drop, waken'd by his song,
  Peeps tremblingly forth,
From her bed of cold still slumber,
  To gaze upon the earth.
For the merry voice above her
  Seem'd a herald of the Spring,
As o'er the sleeping flowers
  Blithe robin came to sing—
"Up, up! my lady snow-drop,
  No longer lie in bed,
But dance unto my melody
  And wave your graceful head."

                TWAMLEY.

PIDERWORT. *Anthericum.* Class 6, HEX-ANDRIA. Order: MONOGYNIA. This plant is generally admitted as a border flower. The French have called it *Ephémèrine de Virginie*, because its flowers fade rapidly, they have also made it the emblem of tran-sient happiness. The dead flowers are quickly succeeded by others, from April to the end of October.

TRANSIENT HAPPINESS

Sweet, as the desert-fountain's wave
To lips just cool'd in time to save.

BYRON.

There comes
For ever something between us and what
We deem our happiness.

BYRON.

All who joy would win
Must share it — happiness was born a twin.

BYRON.

Like a frail shadow seen in maze,
Or some bright star shot o'er the ocean,
Is happiness, that meteor's blaze,
For ever fleeting in its motion.
It plays within our fancied grasp,
Like a phantasmagorean shade,
Pursued e'en to the latest grasp,
It still seems hovering in the glade.
'T is but like hope, and hope's at best
A star that leads the weary on,
Still pointing to the unpossess'd,
And palling that it beams upon.

ANON.

TAR-WORT, CATESBY'S. *Aster Gran-diflorus.* Class 19, Syngenesia. Order: Superflua. This North American plant has been made to represent afterthought, because it sends forth its flowers in the month of November, when most others have disappeared.

AFTERTHOUGHT.

What is done cannot be now amended:
Men shall deal unadvisedly sometimes,
Which after-hours give leisure to repent.

Shakspeare.

The drunkard, after all his lavish cups,
Is dry, and then is sober; so at length,
When you awake from this lascivious dream,
Repentance then will follow, like the sting
Placed in the adder's tail.

Webster.

Habitual evils change not on a sudden,
But many days must pass, and many sorrows,
Conscious remorse, and anguish must be felt,
To curb desire, to break the stubborn will,
And work a second nature in the soul,
Ere virtue can resume the place she lost.

Rowe.

High minds of native pride and force,
Most deeply feel thy pangs, remorse!
Fear for their scourge mean villains have;
Thou art the torturer of the brave.

Scott.

Some who offend from a suspicious nature,
Will afterward such fair confession make
As turns e'en the offence into a favour.

Baillie.

TRAWBERRY TREE. *Arbutus Unedo.*
Class 10, Decandria. Order: Monogynia.
"We have few shrubs," says Miss Twamley, in her 'Romance of Nature,' "which
contribute so much and so constantly to the
adornment of our gardens and lawns as
this. Its deep glossy evergreen leaves are
alone beautiful; but when in Autumn these are gemmed with
its clusters of delicate flowers, and the richly-hued ripening fruit,
(which is a year in attaining maturity, and so appears with the
succeeding blossoms,) I know few objects so beautiful as the
Arbutus.

PERSEVERANCE.

See, like a Ladye in a festal garb,
How gaily deck'd she waits the Christmas time!
Her robe of living emerald, that waves
And, shining, rustles in the frost-bright air,
Is garlanded with bunches of small flowers,—
Small bell-shaped flowers, each of an orient pearl
Most delicately modell'd, and just tinged
With faintest yellow, as if, lit within,
There hung a fairy torch in each lamp-flower.
Some have a pinky hue, soft as a shell
Painted by Amphitrite's hands; for they, less white
Than Lilies where they ope, blush e'en to know
That Summer hath a flower more pure than they.
Twamley

Revolt is recreant, when pursuit is brave;
Never to faint, doth purchase what we crave.
Machen.

Perseverance is a Roman virtue,
That wins each god-like act, and plucks success
Even from the spear-proof crest of rugged danger.
Havard.

UNFLOWER. *Helianthus Annuus.* Class 19, Syngenesia. Order: Trigynia. This species of sunflower is a native of Peru and Mexico, where it sometimes grows to the enormous height of twenty feet; and has flowers two feet in breadth. The Helianthus Indicus, or Dwarf Sunflower, is found in Egypt. The remaining species of this genus, 25 in number, are all indigenous to the Western Continent.

LOFTY AND PURE THOUGHTS.

Where rustic taste at leisure trimly weaves
The rose and straggling woodbine to the eaves,
And on the crowded spot that pales enclose
The white and scarlet daisy rears in rows,
Training the trailing peas in clusters neat,
Perfuming evening with a luscious sweet,
And *sunflowers* planting for their gilded show,
That scale the windows' lattice ere they blow,
And, sweet to habitants within the sheds,
Peep through the crystal panes their golden heads.

Clare.

    I know you all, and will awhile uphold
The unyoked humour of your idleness:
Yet herein will I imitate the sun;
Who doth permit the base contagious clouds
To smother up his beauty from the world,
That, when he please again to be himself,
Being wanted, he may be more wonder'd at,
By breaking through the foul and ugly mists
Of vapours, that did seem to strangle him.

Shakspeare.

Faster than spring-time showers, comes thought on thought;
And not a thought, but thinks on dignity.

Shakspeare.

WEET FLAG. *Acorus Calamus.* Class 6, HEXANDRIA. Order: MONOGYNIA. Linnæus considered the Sweet Flags the only native aromatic plant of northern countries. The root has a strong spicy smell, and when dried, is used in medicine with much success. The Turks eat it as a sweetmeat, and consider it preventive of contagion.

FITNESS.

It was the tall, sweet-scented Flag,
　Lay pictured there so true,
I could have deem'd some Fairy hand
　The faithful image drew.

The falchion-leaves, all long and sharp;
　The stem, like a tall leaf too,
Except where, half-way up its side,
　A cone-shaped flower-spike grew,

Like a Lady's finger, taper, long,
　From end to end array'd
In close scale-armour, that was all
　Of starry flowers made.

If you could fancy fairy folk
　Would mimic work of ours,
You'd think their dainty fingers here
　Had wrought mosaic flowers.

The tiny petals neatly form'd,
　With geometric skill,
Are each one so exactly shaped,
　Its proper place to fill.

And stamens, like fine golden dust,
　Spangle the flowrets green;
Aught more compact or beautiful
　Mine eyes have never seen!　TWAMLEY.

WEET PEA. *Lathyrus Odoratus.* Class 17, DIADELPHIA. Order: DECANDRIA. The sweet pea is a native of Ceylon and of Sicily. Its fragrance is thought to resemble a mixture of the orange-flower and the rose. It richly merits the appellation of *sweet*. The form of the flower is peculiarly graceful.

DEPARTURE.

Put by thy work, dear mother;
  Dear mother come with me,
For I've found within the garden,
  The beautiful sweet-pea!

And bending on their stalks, mother,
  Are roses white and red;
And pale-stemm'd balsams all a-blow,
  On every garden-bed.

Put by thy work, I pray thee,
  And come out, mother dear!
We used to buy these flowers,
  But they are growing here!

Oh, mother! little Amy,
  Would have loved these flowers to see;—
Dost remember how we tried to get
  For her a pink sweet-pea?

Dost remember how she loved
  Those rose-leaves pale and sere!
I wish she had but lived to see
  The lovely roses here!

Put by thy work, dear mother,
  And wipe those tears away!
And come into the garden
  Before 't is set of day!

                    HOWITT.

WEET SULTAN, or CENTAURY. *Centaurea Moschata.* Class 19, SYNGENESIA. Order: FRUSTRANEA. This honey-smelling flower, from the Persian fields, as well as " the corn-flower blue," of our own arable lands, is made the happy emblem of felicity.

Oh! happiness of sweet retired content,
To be at once secure and innocent.
DENHAM.

FELICITY.

All the good we have rests in the mind ;
By whose proportions only we redeem
Our thoughts from out confusion, and do find
The measure of ourselves, and of our powers:
And that all happiness remains confined
Within the kingdom of this breast of ours.
DANIEL.

That happiness does the longest thrive,
Where joys and griefs have turns alternative.
HERRICK.

'T is with our souls
As with our eyes, that after a long darkness
Are dazzled at th' approach of sudden light;
When i' th' midst of fears we are surprised
With unexpected happiness; the first
Degrees of joy are mere astonishment.
DENHAM.

On earth he first beheld
Our two first parents, yet the only two
Of mankind in the happy garden placed,
Reaping immortal fruits of joy and love,
Uninterrupted joy — unrivall'd love.
MILTON.

WEET WILLIAM. *Dianthus Barbatus.* Class 10, Decandria. Order: Digynia. This is a species of pink, a native of Germany. It is much cultivated in our rural gardens, and on account of the brilliancy of its flowers and its agreeable fragrance is deservedly a great favourite with children. The firmness and solidity of its bunches of flowers make it a safe plaything for them.

CHILDHOOD.

Sporting through the forest wide;
Playing by the water-side;
Wandering o'er the heathy fells;
Down within the woodland dells;
All among the mountains wild,
Dwelleth many a little child!
In the baron's hall of pride;
By the poor man's dull fireside:
'Mid the mighty, 'mid the mean,
Little children may be seen,
Like the flowers that spring up fair,
Bright and countless, everywhere!

In the far isles of the main;
In the desert's lone domain;
In the savage mountain glen,
'Mong the tribes of swarthy men;
Wheresoe'er a foot hath gone:
Wheresoe'er the sun hath shone
On a league of peopled ground,
Little children may be found!

Blessings on them! they in me
Move a kindly sympathy,
With their wishes, hopes, and fears;
With their laughter and their tears;
With their wonder so intense,
And their small experience!   How TT.

YCAMORE. *Acer Pseuda-platanus.* Class 23, POLYGAMIA. Order: MONŒCIA. There are two varieties of the sycamore tree, one with broader leaves, and one of which the leaves are variegated. The timber is very close and compact, easily cut, and not liable either to splinter or to warp. Sometimes it is of uniform colour, and sometimes it is very beautifully curled and mottled. In the latter state, as it takes a fine polish, and bears varnishing well, it is much used for certain parts of musical instruments.

WOODLAND BEAUTY.

Nor less attractive is the woodland scene,
Diversified with trees of every growth,
Alike, yet various. Here the grey smooth trunks
Of ash, or lime, or beech, distinctly shine
Within the twilight of their distant shades;
There, lost behind a rising ground, the wood
Seems sunk, and shorten'd to its topmost boughs.
No tree in all the groves but has its charms,
Though each its hue peculiar, paler some,
And of a wannish grey; the willow such,
And poplar that with silver lines his leaf,
And ash, far stretching his umbrageous arm;
Of deeper green the elm: and deeper still,
Lord of the wood, the long-surviving oak.
Some glossy-leaved, and shining in the sun,
The maple, and the beech of oily nuts
Prolific, and the lime at dewy eve
Diffusing odours: nor unnoted pass
The *sycamore,* capricious in attire,
Now green, now tawny, and ere autumn yet
Have changed the wood, in scarlet honours bright.

COWPER.

YRINGA, or MOCK ORANGE. *Philadelphus.* Class 12, Icosandria. Order: Monogynia. This fragrant flower is made the emblem of memory, because when once we inhale its penetrating odour, it continues to dwell on the sense for a considerable time.

MEMORY.

Hail, memory hail! in thy exhaustless mine;
From age to age unnumber'd treasures shine!
Thought and her shadowy brood thy call obey,
And place and time are subjects to thy sway!
Thy pleasures most we feel when most alone,
The only pleasure we can call our own.

ROGERS.

Lull'd in the countless chambers of the brain,
Our thoughts are link'd by many a hidden chain;
Awake but one, and lo, what myriads rise!
Each stamps its image as the other flies!
Each, as the various avenues of sense
Delight or sorrow to the soul dispense,
Brightens or fades; yet all, with magic art,
Control the latent fibres of the heart.
As studious *Prospero's* mysterious spell
Drew every subject-spirit to his cell;
Each, at thy call, advances or retires,
As judgment dictates, or the scene inspires.

ROGERS.

      Through the shadowy past,
Like a tomb-searcher, memory ran,
Lifting each shroud that time had cast
O'er buried hopes.

MOORE.

AMARISK. *Tamarix.* Class 5, PENIAN-
DRIA. Order: TRIGYNIA. It was a custom with the Romans, to put wreaths of
this flexible plant on the heads of crimi-
nals; and hence they mention it as the accursed or unhappy tamarisk, from which
we have devised the emblem.

Criminal love engenders deeds of wickedness that too frequently deserve the wreath of tamarisk.

CRIME.

All have not offended:
For those that were, it is not square to take
On those that are, revenge: crimes, like to lands,
Are not inherited.
SHAKSPEARE.

Where sits the offence,
Let the fault's punishment be derived from thence.
MIDDLETON.

Nor custom, nor example, nor vast numbers
Of such as do offend, make less the sin;
For each particular crime a strict account
Will be exacted; and that comfort, which
The damn'd pretend, follows in misery,
Takes nothing from their torments: ev'ry one
Must suffer in himself the measure of
His wickedness.
MASSINGER.

The laws are sinfully contrived. Justice
Should weigh the present crime, not future
Inference on deeds; but now they cheapen
Blood; 't is spilt
To punish the example, not the guilt.
DAVENANT

ANSY. *Tanacetum.* Class 19, SYNGENE-
SIA. Order: SUPERFLUA. This balsamic
plant, so celebrated of old, is made the emblem of resistance, because it was supposed
to act against contagion.

Since you can love, and yet your error see,
The same resistless power may plead for me.

DRYDEN.

RESISTANCE.

Before my door the box-edged border lies,
Where flowers of mint, and thyme, and tansy rise.

SCOTT.

I pr'ythee take thy fingers from my throat;
For though I am not splenetive and rash,
Yet have I in me something dangerous,
Which let thy wisdom fear. Hold off thy hand.

SHAKSPEARE.

Why, I will fight with him upon this theme
Until my eyelids will no longer wag.

SHAKSPEARE.

Must I give way and room to your rash choler?
Shall I be frighted when a madman stares?

SHAKSPEARE.

Neither the king, nor he that loves him best,
The proudest he that holds up Lancaster,
Dares stir a wing, if Warwick stir his bells.
I'll plant Plantagenet, root him up who dares.

SHAKSPEARE.

My ashes, as the Phœnix, may bring forth
A bird that will revenge upon you all:
And, in that hope, I throw mine eyes to heaven,
Scorning whate'er you can afflict me with.

SHAKSPEARE.

EASEL. *Dipsacus.* Class 4, TETRANDRIA. Order: MONOGYNIA. The flowers of the teasel are bristled with long sharp thorns, and the whole plant has an air or severity; yet it is useful and beautiful. The clothiers use it to raise the nap upon woollen cloths, by means of the chaffs on the heads.

MISANTHROPY.

With purple blooms the Teasel deck'd,
Concentrated in an oval crown;
But not like him of more renown,
Arm'd with the bended awns, that pull
Through the close web the knotted wool,
Raise the soft downy nap, and smooth
The texture with tenacious tooth.
Nor skilful art a tool has plann'd,
To match that gift of Nature's hand.

MANT.

Be abhorr'd
All feasts, societies, and throngs of men!
His semblable, yea, himself, Timon disdains:
Destruction fang mankind!

SHAKSPEARE.

I am Misanthropos, and hate mankind.
For thy part, I do wish thou wert a dog,
That I might love thee something.

SHAKSPEARE.

Nothing I'll bear from thee,
But nakedness, thou detestable town!
Timon will to the woods; where he sha.. find
The unkindest beast more kinder than mankind.

SHAKSPEARE.

 HISTLE. *Carduus.* Class 19, Syngene-
sia. Order: Polygamia Æqualis. This
prickly, though somewhat graceful weed,
has given its title to a Scotch order of
knighthood. It might be said *the* Scotch
order, *par eminence;* as it also bears the
name of St. Andrew, the patron saint of
that nation. The collar is of gold, interlaced with flowers of the
thistle, and bears the following motto: " *Nemo me impune laces-
sit.*" None shall annoy me with impunity.

AUSTERITY.

As Cupid was flying about one day,
With the flowers and zephyrs in wanton play,
    He 'spied in the air,
    Floating here and there,
A winged seed of the thistle-flower,
And merrily chased it from bower to bower.

And young Love cried to his playmates, " See,
I've found the true emblem-flower for me,
    For I am as light
    In my wavering flight
As this feathery star of soft thistle-down,
Which by each of you zephyrs about is blown.

See, how from a Rose's soft warm blush
It flies, to be caught in a bramble bush;—
    And as oft do I,
    In my wand'rings, hie
From beauty to those who have none, I trow;
Reckless as thistle-down, on I go."

So the sly little god still flits away
'Mid earth's loveliest flow'rets, day by day;
    And oh! maidens fair,
    Never weep, nor care
When his light wings waft him beyond your power,
Think — 'tis only the down of the thistle-flower.
                    Twamley.

HORN APPLE. *Datura.* Class 5, Pentandria. Order: Monogynia. The flowers of the datura languish beneath their
sombre and drooping foliage while the sun
shines; but at the approach of night they
put forth, and are reanimated. Then they
display their charms and unfold those im-
mense bell-shaped petals which nature has formed of ivory and
stained with purple, and to which she has confided a perfume
that attracts and invigorates, but is so dangerous, that it produces ebriety and hysterics, even in the open air, on those who
respire it.

DECEITFUL CHARMS.

Oh, what a wild and wayward child am I! —
Like the hungry fool, that in his moody fit
Dash'd from his lips his last delicious morsel.
I'll see her once, Bianca, and but once;
And then a rich and breathing tale I'll tell her
Of our full happiness. If she be angel,
'T will be a gleam of Paradise to her,
And she'll smile at it one of those soft smiles,
That makes the air seem sunny, blithe, and balmy.
If she be devil —— Nay, but that's too ugly;
The fancy doth rebel at it, and shrink
As from a serpent in a knot of flowers.
Devil and Aldabella! — Fie! — They sound
Like nightingales and screech-owls heard together.
What! must I still have tears to kiss away? —
I will return — Good night! — It is but once.
See, thou'st the taste o' my lips now at our parting;
And when we meet again, if they be tainted,
Thou shalt — oh no, thou shalt not, canst not hate me.
                                          Milman.

HYME. *Thymus.* Class 14, DIDYNAMIA. Order: GYMNOSPERMIA. The active qualities of this plant are duly appreciated by epicures, since it excites and rouses their appetites, by rendering every dish savoury in which it is used. We are told, that the highest flavoured venison is always found where this penetrating herb abounds. Bees seek it with great activity: the honey of Athens was esteemed the best in the world, on account of the thyme which grew on the hills which surrounded that city.

> With shepherds on the thyming downs,
> I love to pass the summer's day.
> > WILLIAMS.

ACTIVITY

> O'er fringed heaths, wide lawns, and mountain steeps,
> With silent step the artful Thyma creeps,
> Unfolds with fragrant bloom her purple flowers,
> And leads with frolic hand the circling hours.
> > ROWDEN.

> Wise men ne'er sit and wail their loss,
> But cheerly seek how to redress their harm.
> > SHAKSPEARE.

> Take the instant way;
> For honour travels in a strait so narrow,
> Where one but goes abreast: keep then the path:
> For emulation hath a thousand sons,
> That one by one pursue: if you give way,
> Or edge aside from the direct forthright,
> Like to an enter'd tide, they all rush by,
> And leave you hindmost.
> > SHAKSPEARE.

REFOIL, or PURPLE CLOVER. *Trifo-lium pratense.* Class 17, DIADELPHIA. Or-der: DECANDRIA. The provident husband-man lays up a good store of clover hay for the subsistence of his cattle during the winter months : his earliest spring pastures are also covered with this nutritious plant, which ensures both himself and his stock " a bed of clover."

The great changes which have taken place in agricultural transactions proves the justness of Atterbury's remark, that " a very prosperous people, flushed with great successes, are seldom so pious, so humble, so just, or so provident, as to perpetuate their happiness."

Dryden says,

> Some men, instructed by the lab'ring ant,
> Provide against th' extremities of want.

The use of trefoil in armorial bearings is of great antiquity. The Dutch clover, *Trifolium repens,* is dedicated to St. Patrick it being the shamrock of the Irish.

PROVIDENCE.

> Just as a mother, with sweet pious face,
> Yearns towards her children from her seat,
> Gives one a kiss, another an embrace,
> Takes this upon her knee, that on her feet;
> And while from actions, looks, complaints, pretences,
> She learns their feelings and their various will,
> To this a look, to that a word dispenses,
> And whether stern or smiling, loves them still : —
> So Providence for us, high, infinite,
> Makes our necessities its watchful task,
> Hearkens to all our prayers, helps all our wants :
> And even if it denies what seems our right,
> Either denies because 't would have us ask,
> Or seems but to deny, or in denying grants.
>   ANON.

TRUMPET FLOWER, ASH-LEAVED. *Bignonia Radicans.* Class 14, DIDYNAMIA. Order: ANGIOSPERMIA. Separations are eagerly announced by the trumpets of scandal and ill-nature, who by their discordant sounds, frequently prevent the possibility of a re-union.

The gay corollas of this North American plant drop off, leaving the pistilum destitute of protection, and hence it is presumed the emblem was devised, for where attachment is so slight, separation becomes easy.

SEPARATION.

Alas, for my weary and care-haunted bosom! —
  The spells of the spring-time arouse it no more,
The song in the wild-wood — the sheen of the blossom —
  The fresh-swelling fountain — their magic is o'er!
When I list to the streams — when I look on the flowers,
  They tell of the Past, with so mournful a tone,
That I call up the throngs of my long-vanish'd hours,
  And sigh that their transports are over and gone.

From the wide-spreading earth — from the limitless heaven,
  There have vanish'd an eloquent glory and gleam;
To my veil'd mind no more is the influence given,
  Which coloureth life with the hues of a dream.
The bloom-purpled landscape its loveliness keepeth —
  I deem that a light as of old gilds the wave; —
But the eye of my spirit in heaviness sleepeth,
  Or sees but my youth and the visions it gave.
CLARK.

What! keep a week away? Seven days and nights?
Eight score eight hours? and lovers' absent hours,
More tedious than the dial eight score times?
O weary reckoning!
SHAKSPEARE.

UBEROSE. *Polyanthes Tuberosa.* Class 6, HEXANDRIA. Order: MONOGYNIA. The highly odoriferous properties of this eastern flower have caused it to be a representation of voluptuousness in the floral emblems of the Persians. It is a native of Java and Ceylon.

VOLUPTUOUSNESS.

The tuberose, with her silver light,
  That in the garden of Malay,
Is call'd the mistress of the night;
So like a bride, scented and bright,
  She comes out when the sun's away.
MOORE.

Go to your banquet then, but use delight,
So as to rise still with an appetite.
Love is a thing most nice, and must be fed
To such a height; but never surfeited.
What is beyond the mean is ever ill.
HERRICK.

Give me long dreams and visions of content,
Rather than pleasures in a minute spent:
And since I know before, the shedding rose
In that same instant doth her sweetness lose;
Upon the virgin stock still let her dwell,
For me to feast my longings with her smell.
Those are but counterfeits of joy at best,
Which languish soon as brought unto the test,
Nor can I hold it worth his pains, who tries
To inn that harvest which by reaping dies.
KING.

ULIP TREE. *Liriodendron Tulipifera.*
Class 13, POLYANDRIA. Order: POLYGYNIA.
The tulip-tree, improperly but very commonly called poplar, is abundant in fertile soils, throughout the middle and western states. It grows to the height of 80 or 100 feet, with a trunk three feet and upwards in diameter. The wood is of excellent quality, and is used for a great variety of purposes, even forming an article of export to the north. In the west it supplies the place of the pine, and red and white cedars.

RURAL HAPPINESS.

Ye green-robed Dryads, oft at dusky eve
By wondering shepherds seen, to forest brown,
To unfrequented meads, and pathless wilds,
Lead me from gardens deck'd with art's vain pomps.
Can gilt alcoves, can marble-mimic gods,
Parterres embroider'd, obelisks, and urns
Of high relief: can the long, spreading lake,
Or vista lessening to the sight; can Stow,
With all her Attic fanes, such raptures raise,
As the thrush-haunted copse, where lightly leaps
The fearful fawn the rustling leaves along,
And the brisk squirrel sports from bough to bough,
While from an hollow oak, whose naked roots
O'erhang a pensive rill, the busy bees
Hum drowsy lullabies? The bards of old,
Fair Nature's friends, sought such retreats, to charm
Sweet Echo with her songs; oft, too, they met
In summer evenings, near sequester'd bowers,
Or mountain-nymph, or muse, and eager learn'd
The moral strains she taught to mend mankind.
                               WARTON.

 ULIP. *Tulipa.* Class 6, Hexandria. Order: Monogynia. On the banks of the Bosphorus the tulip is the emblem of inconstancy; but it is also the symbol of the most violent love. The wild tulip is found in the fields of Byzantium, with its crimson petals and golden heart.

A DECLARATION OF LOVE.

Now for madcap Isabel —
What shall suit her, pr'ythee tell?
Isabel is brown and wild;
Will be evermore a child;
Is all laughter, all vagary,
Has the spirit of a fairy.
Are you grave? — The gipsy sly
Turns on you her merry eye,
And you laugh, despite your will.
Isabel is never still,
Always doing, never done,
Be it mischief, work, or fun.
Isabel is short and brown,
Soft to touch as eider-down;
Temper'd like the balmy south,
With a rosy, laughing mouth;
Cheeks just tinged with peachy red,
And a graceful Hebe-head;
Hair put up in some wild way,
Deck'd with a hedge-rose's spray.
Now, where is the bud or bell
That may match with Isabel?

Streaky tulip, jet and gold,
Dearly priced whenever sold;
Rich in colour, low and sweet,
This for Isabel is meet.

HOWITT.

USSILAGE, SWEET-SCENTED. *Tussilago Fragrans.* Class 19, SYNGENESIA. Order: SUPERFLUA. That a European plant of such an exquisite fragrance should have remained unknown until the nineteenth century, was sufficient to have induced M. Villan when he discovered it, to exclaim, " *On vous rendra justice.*"

YOU SHALL HAVE JUSTICE.

As thou urgest justice, be assured,
Thou shalt have justice, more than thou desirest.

SHAKSPEARE.

I beseech you,
Wrest once the law to your authority:
To do a great right, do a little wrong.

SHAKSPEARE.

Impartial are our eyes and ears;
Were he my brother, nay, my kingdom's heir,
Now by my sceptre's awe I make a vow,
Such neighbour nearness to our sacred blood
Should nothing privilege him, nor partialize
The unstooping firmness of my upright soul.

SHAKSPEARE.

Yet show some pity.
Angelo. — I show it most of all, when I show justice;
For then I pity those I do not know,
Which a dismiss'd offence would after gall;
And do him right, that, answering one foul wrong,
Lives not to act another.

SHAKSPEARE.

Justice, like lightning, ever should appear
To few men's ruin, but to all men's fear.

SWETNAM.

ALERIAN. *Valeriana Rubra.* Class 2, DIANDRIA. Order: MONOGYNIA. This plant propagates itself with equal facility in the rich borders of the parterre, or in the dry crevices of old walls, hence the emblem. It was formerly called *Setewale.* Chaucer says,

Ther springen herbes grete and smale,
The Licoris and the Setewale.

ACCOMMODATING DISPOSITION.

Kindness in women, not their beauteous looks,
Shall win my love.

SHAKSPEARE.

What would you have? your gentleness shall force
More than your force move us to gentleness.

SHAKSPEARE.

What thou wilt,
Thou rather shalt enforce it with thy smile,
Than hew tu't with thy sword.

SHAKSPEARE.

You may ride us
With one soft kiss a thousand furlongs, ere
With spur we heat an acre.

SHAKSPEARE.

When your head did but ache,
I knit my handkerchief about your brows,
(The best I had, a princess wrought it me,)
And I did never ask it you again:
And with my hand at midnight held your head;
And, like the watchful minutes to the hour,
Still and anon cheer'd up the heavy time;
Saying, what lack you? and, where lies your grief?

SHAKSPEARE.

ENUS'S FLY-TRAP. *Dionæa muscipula.*
Class 10, DECANDRIA. Order: MONOGYNIA.
The Dionæa muscipula, for there is only one
species, possesses a most curious apparatus
for entrapping insects. The genus is somewhat allied to the Silene or Catchfly, and
bears at the extremity of each of its long
green leaves, which lie spreading on the ground, a pair of large
thick, fleshy lobes, united at their base, and fringed at the mar-
gins with a row of long and slender spines. One might fancy
that this plant gave the first idea of our rat-trap, and its mode of
operating is very nearly the same. No sooner does a fly alight
upon the centre between the two lobes, than these suddenly con-
verge, the spines meet and clasp one within another, and the poor
insects suffers imprisonment and death. The same effect is produced by touching these lobes with a pin, a straw, or any small
object; but this is chiefly observable in fine warm weather; the
contractile power being very weak in winter. Sir J. E. Smith
is decidedly of opinion that these decaying carcases are serviceable to the plant by administering a peculiar air to it; and
M'Knight, a nurseryman, near London, found that a growing
specimen of Dionæa, upon whose leaves he laid fine filaments of
raw beef, was much more luxuriant in its growth than an individual not so treated.

DECEIT.

What man so wise, what earthly wit so ware,
As to descry the crafty cunning train,
By which deceit doth mask in visor fair,
And cast her colours dyed deep in grain,
To seem like truth, whose shape she well can feign,
And fitting gestures to her purpose frame,
The guiltless man with guile to entertain?

SPENSER.

Ah, that deceit should steal such gentle shapes,
And with a virtuous visor hide deep vice!

SHAKSPEARE.

ERVAIN. *Verbena.* Class 2, DIANDRIA. Order: MONOGYNIA. In superstitious ages this plant was not only used in religious ceremonies, but was thought to possess the power of repelling witches and enchanters.

A rev'rent fear, such superstition reigns
Among the rude, ev'n then possess'd the swains.
DRYDEN.

In ancient times the ambassadors or heralds-at-arms wore crowns of vervain when they went to denounce war, or give defiance to their enemies.

A wreath of vervain heralds wear,
Amongst our garlands named,
Being sent that dreadful news to bear,
Offensive war proclaim'd.
DRAYTON.

SUPERSTITION.

England a happy land we know,
Where follies naturally grow,
Where without culture they arise;
And tow'r above the common size;
England, a fortune-telling host,
As num'rous as the stars could boast,
Matrons, who toss the cup, and see
The grounds of fate in grounds of tea.
CHURCHILL.

Gypsies, who ev'ry ill can cure,
Except the ill of being poor,
Who charms 'gainst love and agues sell,
Who can in hen-roost set a spell,
Prepared by arts, to them best known,
To catch all feet except their own,
Who as to fortune can unlock it,
As easily as pick a pocket.
CHURCHILL.

IOLET. *Viola.* Class 5, Pentandria. Order: Monogynia. Ion, the Greek name of this flower, is traced by some etymologists to Ia, the daughter of Midas, who was betrothed to Atys, and changed by Diana into a violet, to hide her from Apollo. The beautiful modest flower still retains the bashful timidity of the nymph, partially concealing itself amidst foliage from the garish gaze of the sun. Hence it has been ingeniously given as a device to an amiable and witty lady of a timid and reserved disposition, surrounded with the motto—*Il faut me chercher*—I must be sought after.

MODESTY.

Sweet violets, Love's paradise, that spread
Your gracious odours, which you couched bear
　　Within your paly faces,
Upon the gentle wing of some calm-breathing wind
　　That plays amidst the plain;
　　If, by the favour of propitious stars, you gain
Such grace as in my lady's bosom place to find,
　　Be proud to touch those places.　　　　Scott.

　　　　I know thou art oft
　　　　　Pass'd carelessly by,
　　　　And the hue so soft
　　　　　Of thine azure eye
Gleams unseen, unsought, in its leafy bower,
While the heartless prefer some statelier flower
That they eagerly cull, and, when faded, fling
Away with rude hand, as a worthless thing.
Not such is *thy* fate: not thy beauty's gift
Alone bids thee from thy bower be reft;
Not thy half-closing, dewy, and deep blue eye;
But the charm that doth not with beauty die.
'T is thy mild, soft fragrance makes thee so dear,
Thou loveliest gem of the floral year!　　Twamley.

IOLET, WHITE. *Viola Lactea.* Class 5, PENTANDRIA. Order: MONOGYNIA. Candour precedes modesty, of which the blue violet is frequently used as the emblem. The white violet is the same flower, still clothed in the robes of innocence. It is rarer than the common violet, and as pretty.

CANDOUR.

Make my breast
Transparent as pure crystal, that the world,
Jealous of me, may see the foulest thought
My heart does hold.

BUCKINGHAM.

You talk to me in parables:
You may have known that I'm no wordy man;
Fine speeches are the instruments of knaves
Or fools that use them, when they want good sense;
But honesty
Needs no disguise nor ornament: be plain.

OTWAY.

The brave do never shun the light;
Just are their thoughts, and open are their tempers;
Truly without disguise they love or hate;
Still are they found in the fair face of day,
And heaven and men are judges of their actions.

ROWE.

'T is great—'t is manly to disdain disguise;
It shows our spirit, or it proves our strength.

YOUNG.

Her words are trusty heralds to her mind.

FORD.

ALL-FLOWER. *Cheiranthus.* Class 15, TETRADYNAMIA. Order: SILIQUOSA. We are told that the minstrels and troubadours of former days carried a branch of wall-flower as the emblem of an affection which continues through all the vicissitudes of time, and survives every misfortune. During the reign of terror in France, the violent populace precipitated themselves towards the abbey of St. Denis, to disinter the ashes of their kings and scatter them to the winds. The barbarians, after breaking open the sacred tombs, were affrighted at the sacrilege, and went and hid their spoil in an obscure corner behind the choir of the church, where they were forgotten amid the horrors of the revolution. The poet, Treneuil, some time after visited the spot, and found the sculptured fragments covered with the wall-flower.

FIDELITY IN MISFORTUNE.

Why this flower is now call'd so,
List, sweet maids, and you shall know.
Understand, this firstling was
Once a brisk and bonny lasse,
(Kept as close as Danaë was;)
Who a sprightly springall loved,
And, to have it fully proved,
Up she got upon a wall,
Tempting down to slide withall;
But the silken twist untied,
So she fell, and bruised, she died.
Love, in pity of the deed,
And her loving lucklesse speed,
Changed her to this plant, we call
Now, the Flower of the Wall.
HERRICK.

ALL SPEEDWELL. *Veronica Arvensis.*
Class 2, DIANDRIA. Order: MONOGYNIA.
This beautiful plant, that attaches itself to old walls,

" And decks his branch with blossoms over all;"

reflecting in its petals the azure of the heavens, is made the symbol of fidelity.

Its relative, the common speedwell, *veronica officinalis*, stands as the emblem of resemblance; the Greek name of speedwell meaning true image.

> Fairest resemblance of thy Maker fair,
> Thee, all things living gaze on.   MILTON.

FIDELITY.

How shall I see those pleasant fields again,
  When I shall miss, whene'er mine eyes I bend,
  The look, the smile, of that beloved friend,
Who made this world, so oft a world of pain,
  To me, oh, more than happy! — Every scene
Was here familiar, from life's early morn,
The trees, the tow'r, the cliff, the hill-top thorn;
  And, long-accustom'd on my arm to lean,
I oft have heard her say, that "search around
The earth, no spot more blissful could be found."

Thy path is now beyond those fading hills,
And many a fear my anxious bosom fills,
  Which Fancy shapes in solitude! but yet,—
I know thy warm and honest heart replies,
(A tear of accusation in thine eyes)
  "Oh! can I ever these or thee forget?"
Well! be thou happy! but I fear, the day
Will come, when I with aching heart shall say
(Watching the melancholy show'rs of eve),
"Why didst thou ever these green valleys leave?"
                            BOWLES.

ALNUT, BLACK. *Juglans Nigra.* Class 21, Monœcia. Order: Polyandria. The black walnut is found in most parts of the United States, the extreme north and north-east excepted, and the low district of the southern States, where its absence seems to be owing to the nature of the soil, which is either too sandy or too wet. It requires a deep and fertile soil, and the trunk sometimes attains the diameter of 6 or 7 feet. It is one of our largest trees, and yields to none in the majesty of its appearance. The nuts are sold in our markets, and the wood is serviceable for a variety of purposes.

INTELLECT.

The walnut, then, approach'd, more large and tall,
His fruit, we a nut but some an acorn call:
Jove's acorn, which does no small praise confess;
To have call'd it man's ambrosia had been best.
Nor can this head-like nut, shaped like the brain,
Within, be said that form by change to gain,
Or caryon call'd by learn'd Greeks in vain;
For membranes soft as silk her kernel bind,
Whereof the inmost is of tenderest kind,
Like those which on the brain of man we find;
All which are in a seam-join'd shell enclosed;
Which of this brain the skull may be supposed:
This very skull enveloped is again
In a green coat, his pericranium:
Lastly, that no objection may remain,
To thwart her near alliance to the brain,
She nourishes the hair, remembering how
Herself, deform'd, without her leaves does show;
On barren scalps she makes fresh honours grow.

ANON.

ATER LILY. *Nymphæa Alba.* Class 13, POLYANDRIA. Order: MONOGYNIA. The Egyptians have consecrated to the sun, the god of eloquence, the flower of the Nymphæa Lotus. This flower closes at evening, and reclines on the bosom of the lake, from the setting of the sun, until the rising of that splendid orb on the succeeding morn. Flowers of the lotus are inwoven in the head-dress of Osiris. The Indian gods also are frequently represented on the waters as seated on this flower; it is supposed that this allegory may be understood as an allusion to the fable of the world rising from the midst of the waters.

ELOQUENCE.

Oh come to the river's rim, come with us there,
For the white Water Lily is wondrous fair,
With her large broad leaves on the stream afloat,
Each one a capacious fairy-boat.
The swan among flowers! How stately ride
Her snow-white leaves on the glittering tide!
And the Dragon-fly gallantly stays to sip
A kiss of dew from her goblet's lip.

TWAMLEY.

O eloquence! thou violated fair!
How art thou woo'd, and won to either bed
Of right or wrong! O when injustice folds thee,
Dost thou not curse thy charms for pleasing him,
And blush at conquest?

HAVARD.

Thy words had such a melting flow,
And spoke of truth so sweetly well,
They dropp'd like heaven's serenest snow,
And all was brightness where they fell!

MOORE.

HEAT. *Triticum.* Class 3, TRIANDRIA. Order: DIGYNIA. Floral hieroglyphics have not a more appropriate emblem than that of representing riches by this gift of Ceres.

Without content no man can be rich, and it will always be found that there is a greater proportion of wealthy poor people, than of rich in content.

> What riches give us, let us first enquire,
> Meat, fire, and clothes; what more? meat, clothes, and fire.
>
> POPE.

RICHES.

> Of golden wheat, the strength of human life.
>
> PHILIPS.

> Why dost thou heap up wealth, which thou must quit,
> Or what is worse, be left by it?
> Why dost thou load thyself when thou'rt to fly,
> Oh, man! ordain'd to die?
> Why dost thou build up stately rooms on high,
> Thou who art under ground to lie?
> Thou sow'st and plantest, but no fruit must see,
> For death, alas! is reaping thee.
>
> COWLEY.

> Riches, like insects, while conceal'd they lie,
> Wait but for wings, and in their seasons fly;
> To whom can riches give repute and trust,
> Content or pleasure, but the good and just?
> Judges and senates have been bought for gold,
> Esteem and love are never to be sold.
>
> POPE.

> Can wealth give happiness? look round, and see
> What gay distress! what splendid misery!
> Whatever fortune lavishly can pour,
> The mind annihilates, and calls for more.
>
> YOUNG.

HITE OAK. *Quercus Alba.* Class 21, MONŒCIA. Order: POLYANDRIA. The White Oak is found in most parts of the United States, but in general too thinly scattered to supply even the local demand. It abounds most in the middle States, and particularly in west Pennsylvania and Virginia. Of all the American oaks, it affords the best timber for general purposes, and that most frequently used, being strong, durable, and of large size; inferior, indeed, to the English oak in strength and durability, though more elastic.

INDEPENDENCE.

I care not, Fortune, what you me deny:
You cannot rob me of free Nature's grace:
You cannot shut the windows of the sky
Through which Aurora shows her brightening face;
You cannot bar my constant feet to trace
The woods and lawns, by living stream, at eve:
Let health my nerves and finer fibres brace,
And I their toys to the great children leave:
Of fancy, reason, virtue, nought can me bereave.

THOMSON.

Thy spirit, Independence, let me share,
Lord of the lion-heart and eagle-eye,
Thy steps I follow with my bosom bare,
Nor heed the storm that howls along the sky.

Deep in the frozen regions of the north,
A goddess violated brought thee forth,
Immortal Liberty! whose look sublime
Hath bleach'd the tyrant's cheek in every varying clime.

SMOLLETT.

For me, my lot is what I sought; to be,
In life or death, the fearless and the free.

BYRON.

HORTLE-BERRY. *Vaccinium Myrtillus.* Class 8, OCTANDRIA. Order: MONOGYNIA. This emblem of treason is only found on dreary heaths and mountainous situations, where its fruit has often been used to disguise the face of the proscribed. The Whortleberry is probably more generally diffused over the United States than any other berry or fruit. It is a favourite at all tables.

TREASON.

Come, stain your face with whortle-berry.
ANON.

Smooth runs the water, where the brook is deep,
And in his simple show he harbours treason.
The fox barks not, when he would steal the lamb.
SHAKSPEARE.

He therefore wisely cast about,
All ways he could, t' ensure his throat,
And hither came, t' observe and smoke
What courses other riskers took;
And to the utmost do his best
To save himself, and hang the rest.
BUTLER.

How safe is treason, and how sacred ill,
When none can sin against the people's will;
Where crowds can wink and no offence be known,
Since in another's guilt they find their own.
DRYDEN.

      Is there not some chosen curse,
Some hidden thunder in the stores of heaven
Red with uncommon wrath, to blast the man,
Who owes his greatness to his country's ruin?
ADDISON.

ILLOW.   *Salix Babylonica.*   Class 22, Diœcia.   Order: Diandria.   The botanical name *salix* is derived from two Celtic words, *sal*, near, and *lis*, water.   The willows all bear catkins, or long bunches of blossoms, some of which are very showy and handsome and sweet-scented.   The willows are not a very ornamental tribe, but we are so accustomed to see them growing in pleasant places, beside romantic streams, that they become beautiful by association.

FORSAKEN.

The *Watery Willow's* spray, emboss'd
With oval knots of silken down;
Which soon, in form of papal crown,
Shall decorate the russet stem
With many a golden diadem.

MANT.

Thus o'er our streams do eastern willows lean
In pensive guise; whose grief-inspiring shade,
Love has to melancholy sacred made.

DELILLE.

To the brook and the willow that heard him complain,
        Ah, willow! willow!
Poor Colin went weeping and told them his pain.

ROWE.

I offered him my company to a willow tree, to make him a garland, as being forsaken; to bind him up a rod, as being worthy to be whipt.

SHAKSPEARE.

In love the sad forsaken wight
The willow garland weareth.

DRAYTON.

ILLOW HERB. *Epilobium.* Class 8, OCT-ANDRIA. Order: MONOGYNIA. This beautiful plant, which flourishes by the water's side, seems to take pleasure in admiring itself in the crystal stream. For this reason it is compared to a vain woman, proud of her own charms. Mr. Loudon says that it is a thriving plant, and will grow anywhere, under the drip of trees, and in smoky cities, parks, &c., and is very showy when in flower.

PRETENSION.

<blockquote>
Appearances deceive,
And this one maxim is a standing rule,—
Men are not what they seem.
</blockquote>

HAVARD.

<blockquote>
Seems, madam! nay, it is; I know not *seems.*
'T is not alone my inky cloak, good mother,
Nor customary suits of solemn black,
Nor windy suspiration of forced breath,
No, nor the fruitful river in the eye,
Nor the dejected 'haviour of the visage,
Together with all forms, modes, shows of grief,
That can denote me truly: These, indeed, seem,
For they are actions that a man might play:
But I have that within, which passeth show;
These, but the trappings and the suits of woe.
</blockquote>

SHAKSPEARE.

<blockquote>
There is a fair behaviour in thee, captain;
And though that nature with a bounteous wall
Doth oft close in pollution, yet of thee
I will believe, thou hast a mind that suits
With this thy fair and outward character.
</blockquote>

SHAKSPEARE.

INTER CHERRY. *Physalis Alkekergi.*
Class 5, PENTANDRIA. Order: MONOGYNIA.
We present this berry as the emblem of
deception, since it assumes all the beauty
of the cherry, in shape, gloss, and colouring, but is entirely destitute of the agreeable taste of the real cherry.

DECEPTION.

He seem'd
For dignity composed and high exploit:
But all was false and hollow.

MILTON.

A villain, when he most seems kind,
Is most to be suspected.

LANSDOWN.

Thou hast prevaricated with thy friend,
By under-hand contrivances undone me;
And while my open nature trusted in thee,
Thou hast stepp'd in between me and my hopes,
And ravish'd from me all my soul held dear.
Thou hast betray'd me.

ROWE.

The man who dares to dress misdeeds,
And colour them with virtue's name, deserves
A double punishment from gods and men.

JOHNSON.

'T is not my talent to conceal my thoughts,
Or carry smiles and sunshine in my face,
When discontent sits heavy at my heart.

ADDISON.

The world's all title-page; there's no contents;
The world's all face; the man who shows his heart
Is hooted for his nudities, and scorn'd.

YOUNG.

OOD SORREL. *Oxalis.* Class 10, Dec-
ANDRIA. Order: PENTAGYNIA. The wood
sorrel, vulgarly called "cuckoo's bread,"
flowers very freely, about Easter. This
pretty little plant shuts its leaves, closes its
corollas, and the flowers hang pendent and
drooping from the stems. They seem to
yield themselves to sleep; but at the first dawn of day we may
say that they are filled with joy, for they throw back their leaves,
and expand their flowers; and we doubt not it is on this account
that peasants have said that they sing the praises of their Creator.

JOY.

Indeed true gladness doth not always speak:
Joy bred, and born but in the tongue, is weak.
JONSON.

Swell, swell, my joys; and faint not to declare
Yourselves as ample, as your causes are.
JONSON.

True joy is only hope put out of fear;
And honour hideth error ev'ry where.
BROOKE.

Wonder and joy so fast together flow,
Their haste to pass, has made their passage slow;
Like struggling waters in a vessel pent,
Whose crowding drops choke up the narrow vent.
HOWARD.

Wise heaven doth see it as fit
In all our joys to give us some alloys,
As in our sorrows comforts: when our sails
Are fill'd with happiest winds, then we most need
Some heaviness to ballast us.
FOUNTAIN.

ORMWOOD. *Artemisia.* Class 19, SYN-GENESIA. Order: SUPERFLUA. Worm-wood is considered the bitterest of plants. Its scientific name, *Absinthus*, is derived from the Greek and signifies — without sweetness. It is, therefore, very appropriately made the emblem of absence; which, according to La Fontaine, is the greatest of evils.

To be separated from those to whom we are devotedly attached, is assuredly one of the severest trials of life; and if that separation be involuntary, or only in obedience to those who have the guardianship of our early years, the wretchedness of absence is enhanced three-fold. There is all the anxiety for the health and comfort of the absent, without any opportunity of offering consolation; for, though "the heart alone knows its own bitterness," we feel that the sympathy of a friend can often alleviate the deepest distress.

ABSENCE.

Her fancy follow'd him through foaming waves
To distant shores, and she would sit and weep
At what a sailor suffers. Fancy, too,
Delusive most where warmest wishes are,
Would oft anticipate his glad return,
And dream of transports she was not to know.
COWPER.

Yes,
The limner's art may trace the absent feature,
And give the eye of distant weeping faith
To view the form of its idolatry;
But oh! the scenes 'mid which they met and parted,
The thoughts — the recollections sweet and bitter,
Th' Elysian dreams of lovers, when they loved,
Who shall restore them?
Less lovely are the fugitive clouds of eve,
And not more vanishing.
MATURIN.

ARROW. *Achillea Millefolium.* Class **19**, SYNGENESIA. Order: SUPERFLUA. Milfoil, or Yarrow, cicatrizes all wounds made by iron. It is said that Achilles, whose name it bears, used it to cure the wounds of Telephus. Its having received from the ancients the name of this celebrated hero renders it a very appropriate emblem of war.

WAR.

It was a dread, yet spirit-stirring sight!
The billows foam'd beneath a thousand oars.
Fast as they land, the red-cross ranks unite,
Legions on legions brightening all the shores.
Then banners rise, and cannon-signal roars,
Then peals the warlike thunder of the drum,
Thrills the loud fife, the trumpet flourish pours,
And patriot hopes awake, and doubts are dumb;
For bold in freedom's cause, the bands of ocean come.
SCOTT.

'T was bustle in the court below,
"Mount and march forward!" forth they go;
Steeds neigh and trample all around,
Steel rings, spears glimmer, trumpets sound.
SCOTT.

Thus while they looked, a flourish proud,
Where mingled trump, and clarion loud,
And fife, and kettle-drum,
And sackbut deep, and psaltery,
And war-pipe with discordant cry,
And cymbal clattering to the sky,
Making wild music bold and high,
Did up the mountain come.
SCOTT.

EW. *Taxus.* Class 21, MONŒCIA. Order: POLYANDRIA. There is in every plant something which either attracts or repels us. The yew tree is considered by all nations to be the emblem of sorrow. Plants are said to die under its shade, and if the weary traveller should sleep under its umbrageous branches his head becomes affected, and he soon feels violently ill. It also exhausts the earth which yields it nourishment. Our ancestors, guided by a natural sentiment, considered it a fit resident in the cemetery, and so destined it to overshade the tomb. They used its wood for bows, lances, and cross-bows; and the Greeks also employed it for the same purposes.

SORROW.

Beneath that yew tree's shade,
  Where heaves the turf in many a mouldering heap,
Each in his narrow cell for ever laid,
  The rude forefathers of the hamlet sleep.
GRAY.

Both you two have
Relation to the grave;
    And where
The fun'rale trump sounds, you are there.

I shall be made
Ere long a fleeting shade;
    Pray come
And doe some honour to my tomb.

Do not deny
My last request, for I
    Will be
Thankful to you, or friends for me.
HERRICK.

INNIA. *Zinnia.* Class 19, SYNGENESIA. Order: POLYGAMIA SUPERFLUA. This flower received its singular name from a German botanist, Dr. John G. Zinn. We have many species of this genus in America. The red is found on the banks of the Mississippi; the yellow is a native of Peru; the scarlet, purple-flowered and slender-flowered, of Mexico.

ABSENCE.

Short absence hurt him more,
And made his wound far greater than before;
Absence not long enough to root out quite
All love, increases love at second sight.

MAY.

I do not doubt his love, but I could wish
His presence might confirm it: when I see
A fire well fed, shoot up its wanton flame,
And dart itself into the face of heaven;
I grant that fire, without a fresh supply,
May for a while be still a fire; but yet
How doth its lustre languish, and itself
Grow dark, if it too long want the embrace
Of its loved pyle? how straight it buried lies
In its own ruins.

MEAD.

O thou that dost inhabit in my breast,
Leave not the mansion so long tenantless;
Lest, growing ruinous, the building fall,
And leave no memory of what it was!
Repair me with thy presence, Sylvia;
Thou gentle nymph, cherish thy forlorn swain.

SHAKSPEARE.

Love reckons hours for months, and days for years;
And every little absence is an age.

DRYDEN.

BOTANY.

BOTANY is the science of plants. It teaches their natural history and intrinsic qualities; and, to facilitate an acquaintance with these particulars, arranges all vegetables in classes, orders, and other subdivisions. This arrangement is called a system. Various systems, or plans of arrangement, have been from time to time proposed; but the sexual system of Linnæus is at present generally received. This naturalist has drawn a continued analogy between the vegetable economy and that of the animal; and has derived all his classes, orders, and genera, from the number, situation, and proportion of the parts of fructification. In twenty-four *classes*, he has comprehended every known genus and species. In considering a plant with a view to its characteristics or distinguishing features, it is divided by Linnæus into the following parts, making so many outlines, to which the attention of the botanical observer must be directed: 1. Root; 2. Trunk; 3. Leaves; 4. Props; 5. Fructification; 6. Inflorescence. 1. The *root* consists of two parts, the *caudex* and the *radicula*. The *caudex*, or stump, is the body or knob of the root from which the trunk and branches ascend, and the fibrous roots descend, and is either solid, bulbous, or tuberous: solid, as in trees and other examples; bulbous, as in tulips, &c.; tuberous, as in potatoes, &c. The *radicula* is the fibrous part of the root, branching from the *caudex*. 2. The *trunk*, which includes the branches, is that part which rises immediately from the *caudex*, is either herbaceous, shrubby, or arborescent, and admits of several other distinctions, according to its shape, substance, surface, &c. 3. The *leaves* are either *simple*, as those that adhere to the branch singly, or *compound*, as when several expand from one footstalk. Leaves are farther described by various terms indicative of their form and outline. 4. The *props*, those external parts which strengthen, support, or defend the plants on which they are found, or serve to facilitate some necessary secretion: as, the *petiolus*, or footstalk of the leaf; the *pedunculus*, or footstalk of the flower; the *stipula*, or husk, that is, the small leaves that generally surround the stalk at its divisions; the *cirrhus*, or tendril; the *pubes*, or down; the *arma*, or defensive weapon, as thorns. 5. The *fructification*, or *mode* of fruit-bearing. 6. The *inflorescence*, or *mode* by which the flowers are joined to the several peduncles.

The various parts of a flower are arranged under distinct heads, consisting of the "Calyx" or Empalement: the "Blossom" or Corolla: "Stamens" or Chives: "Pistils" or Pointals: "Seed Vessels" or Pericarpium, and "Seeds" or Semina. To these are to be added the "Nectary" and "Receptacle." The calyx is formed of one or more green or yellowish-green leaves placed at a small distance from, or close to the blossom. There are different kinds of calyxes, as the perianthium or cup near the flower, in the rose:—the involucrum, remote from the flower, in umbelliferous plants, as is seen in the hemlock and carrot:—the catkin, or amentum, as in the willow or hazel:—the sheath, or spatha, in the snow-drop:—the husk, or gluma, in wheat, oats, and different kinds of grasses:—the veil, or calyptra, covering the fructification of some of the mosses, and resembling an extinguisher:—the curtain, or volva, surrounding the stems, and attached to the pileus, or cap, that spreading part which forms the top of several fungi, and covers the fructification, and which in the common mushroom covers the gills.

The Blossom is that beautifully coloured part of a flower, which principally attracts the attention. It is composed of one or more petals, or blossom-leaves. When it is united in one, as in the Polyanthus or Auricula, it is termed a blossom of one petal, but if it be composed of many parts, it is then said to be a blossom of two, three, or many petals.

The Stamens are slender thread-like substances, generally placed within the blossom, and surrounding the Pistils. It is composed of two parts, the Filament or Thread, and the Anther or Tip, but the latter is the essential.

A Pistil consists of three divisions, the Germen or Seed-bud, the Style or Shaft, and the Summit or Stigma; but the second is often wanting. Some flowers have only one Pistil: others have two, three, four, &c., or more than can easily be counted. The Seed-Vessel, in the newly-opening flower, is called the Germen; but when it enlarges it is termed the Seed-Vessel. Some plants have no appendage of the kind, and then the seeds are uncovered, as in the dead nettle; the cup, however, generally incloses and retains the seeds till they ripen: and in the tribe of grasses, this friendly office is generally performed by what was previously called the blossom. Seeds are sufficiently well known to render a description unnecessary : the part to which they are affixed within the Seed-Vessel, is termed the Receptacle of the seeds.

Nectaries are those parts in a flower which are designed to prepare a sweet nectareous liquor. The tube of the blossom, as in the honey-suckle, frequently answers the purpose; but in many other flowers, there is a peculiar organization for the purpose. At the base of the petal, in the crown imperial, the Nectary is a very peculiar one, containing the liquor, from which, as there are few flowers in a greater or less degree unprovided with it, the little industrious bee derives its honey.

The Receptacle is the seat or base to which the various divisions of a flower are affixed. Thus, if you pull off the Calyx, the Blossoms, the Stamens, the Pistils, and the Seeds or Seed-Vessel, the substance remaining on the top of the stalk is the Receptacle. In many plants it is not particularly striking, but in others it is remarkably so; thus, in the artichoke, after removing the Calyx, the Blossoms, and the bristly substances, the remaining part, so highly esteemed for the table, is the Receptacle.

The Classes are next to be considered, which were, according to the system of Linnæus, divided into twenty-four.

The characters are taken either from the number, length, connexion, or situation of the Stamens.

The first class comprehends all that have a single stamen in each blossom, and this he calls *monandria* (one male); the second class such as have two stamina, called *diandria* (two males);

the third, fourth, and so on, up to the tenth, are named in the same way, *triandria* (three males), *tetrandria* (four males), &c. &c. There being no plants with eleven stamina, and the number not being uniformly twelve in many plants, though there or thereabouts, the eleventh class, called *dodecandria* (twelve males), includes all plants that have from eleven to nineteen inclusive. If the stamina are twenty or more, and are attached to the calyx or corolla, the plants belong to the twelfth class, *icosandria* (twenty males). If above nineteen, and attached to the base of the flower, and not to the calyx or corolla, they are of the class *polyandria* (many males), which is the thirteenth class. Plants with four stamina, two of which are shorter than the other two, are in the fourteenth class, *didynamia* (two powers). Plants with four long and two short stamina constitute the fifteenth class, the *tetradynamia* (four powers). In *monadelphia*, which is the name of the sixteenth class, the threads of the stamina are all united at bottom, but the antheræ are separate. In *diadelphia* the threads are united, not altogether, but in two bodies. In *polyadelphia* they are connected in three or more bodies. If the threads are separate, but the antheræ united, the plant is in the nineteenth class, *syngenesia*. In all the above classes the stamina are distinct, and separate from the pistillum; but where the former grow upon the latter, the plant is of the class *gynandria*, which is the twentieth. Sometimes the stamina are in one blossom, and the pistillum or pistilla in another but on the same plant: in this case they form the class *monœcia* (one house). But if the staminiferous blossom is on one plant, and the pistilliferous on another, it is of the twenty-second class, *diœcia* (two houses). And lastly, if some blossoms have both stamina and pistilla, and others only one or the other, whether on the same plant, or on different plants, they come under the twenty-third class, *polygamia*. These include all vegetables whose flowers are conspicuous. But there are some, as mosses, sea-weeds, mushrooms, &c., whose flowers are inconspicuous, or whose parts of fructification are not stamina and pistilla. These are all arranged together in the twenty-fourth class, called **cryptogamia**.

These 24 classes have been recently reduced to 20, which may be thus arranged with examples under each.

TABLE OF THE CLASSES.

Class.	Stamens in each Flower.	Examples.
1. Monandria - - one		Mares-tail, Parsleypiert.
2. Diandria - - - two		Privet, Sage.
3. Triandria - - three		Yellow Flag, the Grasses.
4. Tetrandria - - four, all of the same length		Plantain, Scabious.
5. Pentandria - - five, the anthers not united		Honeysuckle, Primrose.
6. Hexandria - - six, all of the same ength		Snowdrop, Asparagus.
7. Heptandria - - seven		Horse Chestnut.
8. Octandria - - - eight		Mezereon, Heath, Willowherb.
9. Enneandria - nine		Bay Tree, Flowering Rush.
10. Decandria - - ten, the filaments not united		Campion, Pink, Arbutus.
11. Dodecandria - 12 to 19		Houseleek.
12. Icosandria - - more than 12, fixed to the calyx or petals - -		Hawthorn, Plum, Rose.
13. Polyandria - - 20 to 1000, fixed to the receptacle		Poppy, Larkspur, Anemone.
14. Didynamia - - four, 2 long and 2 short		Ground Ivy, Foxglove.
15. Tetradynamia six, 4 long and 2 short		Cabbage, Wallflower.
16. Monadelphia - the filaments united		Mallow Geranium.
17. Diadelphia - - in 1 or 2 sets, blossoms butterfly-shaped - - -		Pea, Furze, Broom.
18. Polyadelphia - in 3 or more sets		Orange, St. John's Wort.
19. Syngenesia - - 5 stam. anthers united, flowers compound - -		Coltsfoot, Sunflower, Thistle.
20. Cryptogamia - flowers inconspicuous		Fern, Moss, Liverwort, Sea-Weeds, Mushrooms.

A knowledge of the Orders may be very easily attained, by observing that,

In the class Didynamia, they depend upon the seeds having a seed-vessel, or not.

Tetradynamia, upon the shape of the seed-vessel.

Syngenesia, upon the structure of the florets.

Cryptogamia, upon the natural assemblages of plants resembling each other.

And that in all the other classes, excepting Monadelphia, Diadelphia, and Polyadelphia, they depend upon the number of pistils only. In determining the number of pistils, count the styles, as they appear at their bottom part, or base; but if the summits are not supported upon styles, then count the summits.

Recapitulation of the Classes, with their attendant Orders and familiar examples.

Monandria.

Order Monogynia (1 pistil) Common Stonewort.

Digynia . . (2 pistils) Water Fennel.

Tetragynia (4 pistils) Pondweed.

Diandria.

    Order Monogynia (1 pistil) Privet.

        Digynia . . (2 pistils) Sweet-scented Vernal Grass.

Triandria.

    Order Monogynia (1 pistil) Wild Vine.

        Digynia . . (2 pistils) Meadow Foxtail.

        Trigynia . . (3 pistils) Small-water Chickweed.

        Enneagynia (9 pistils) Blackberried Heath.

Tetrandria.

    Order Monogynia (1 pistil) Shepherd's Rod.

        Digynia . . (2 pistils) Chickweed Toadgrass.

        Trigynia . . (3 pistils) Common Box.

        Tetragynia (4 pistils) Common Holly.

Pentandria.

    Order Monogynia (1 pistil) Water Mouse-ear.

        Digynia . . (2 pistils) Common Hop.

        Trigynia . . (3 pistils) Dwarf Elder.

        Tetragynia (4 pistils) Grass of Parnassus.

        Pentagynia (5 pistils) Round-leaved Sundew.

        Polygynia . (many pistils) Little Mouse-ear.

Hexandria.

    Order Monogynia (1 pistil) Common Snowdrop.

        Trigynia . . (3 pistils) Meadow-Saffron.

        Hexagynia (6 pistils) Saracen's Birthwort.

        Polygynia . (many pistils) Water Plantain.

Heptandria.

    Order Monogynia (1 pistil) Chickweed Winter-Green.

Octandria.

    Order Monogynia (1 pistil) Rosebay Willow-Herb.

        Digynia . . (2 pistils) Common Hazel-Nut Tree.

        Trigynia . . (3 pistils) Snake Weed.

        Tetragynia (4 pistils) Water Wort.

Enneandria.

    Order Digynia . . (2 pistils) Dog Mercury.

        Hexagynia (6 pistils) Flowering Rush.

Decandria.

    Order Monogynia (1 pistil) Wild Rosemary.

Digynia .. (2 pistils) London Pride.

Trigynia.. (3 pistils) Greater Stitchwort.

Pentagynia (5 pistils) Cuckoo Flower.

Dodecandria.

Order Monogynia (1 pistil) Floating Hornweed.

Digynia .. (2 pistils) Common Agrimony.

Trigynia.. (3 pistils) Chestnut Tree.

Dodecagynia (12 pistils) Common Houseleek.

Icosandria.

Order Monogynia (1 pistil) Black-Thorn.

Digynia .. (2 pistils) Hawthorn.

Trigynia.. (3 pistils) Mountain Ash.

Pentagynia (5 pistils) Crab Tree.

Polygynia . (many pistils) Common Meadow Sweet.

Although this is called the class of 20 Stamens, because the flowers arranged under it generally contain about that number; yet the classic character is not to be taken merely from the number of stamens, but from a consideration of the following circumstances, which will sufficiently distinguish it both from the preceding and following classes.

Calyx, consisting of one leaf, concave.

Petals, fixed by claws to the inside of calyx.

Stamens, more than 19, standing upon the petals or calyx, (but not upon the receptacle).

Polyandria.

Order Monogynia (1 pistil) Common Celandine.

Digynia .. (2 pistils) Upland Burnet.

Trigynia.. (3 pistils) Wild Larkspur.

Pentagynia (5 pistils) Columbine.

Hexagynia (6 pistils) Water Aloes.

Polygynia . (many pistils) Wood Anemone.

Most of this class are poisonous.

Didynamia.

Order Gymnospermia (seeds uncovered) Red Dead Nettle.

Angiospermia . (seeds covered) Common Eyebright.

The plants in the first order of this class are odoriferous and cephalic: none of them are poisonous.

Tetradynamia.

Order Siloculosa (Pouch, or broad Pod) Horse-radish.
Siliquosa . (long Pod) Wall-flower.

It is necessary to remark, that the flowers of this class have uniformly 4 petals ; an attention to this circumstance will proba-bly save the learner some trouble, as the difference in the length of the stamens is not always very obvious, and especially as the plants of the Hexandria class have none of them 4 petals.

Monadelphia.

Order Triandria . (3 stamens) Juniper Tree.
Decandria . (10 stamens) Wood Cranesbill.
Polyandria (many stamens) Common Mallow.

In this class the filaments are all together at the bottom, but separate at the top. The orders in this and the two following are determined by the number of the stamens.

Diadelphia.

Order Hexandria (6 stamens) Common Fumitory.
Octandria . (8 stamens) Common Milkwort.
Decandria (10 stamens) Common Vetch.

This class comprehends the butterfly-shaped flowers. From the name of this class, the young Botanist will be induced to imagine, that the filaments are always formed into two sets, but this is by no means the case, as in many instances they are united into one set. The butterfly-shape of the blossom will therefore (as in the garden pea) be a more certain guide.

Polyadelphia.

Order Polyandria.   Common St. John's Wort.

Syngenesia.

Order Polygamia Æqualis. Florets furnished with stamens and pistils. Common Sowthistle.
Polygamia Superflua. Florets in the centre, furnished with stamens and pistils, those in the circumference with only pistils. Groundsel.
Polygamia Frustanea. Florets in the centre, furnished with stamens and pistils, those in the circumference without any. Corn-flower.

Polygamia Necessaria. Florets in the centre, furnished with stamens and pistils, but producing no seed. Those in the circumference with only pistils, and producing seed. Marigold.

Polygamia Segregata. (Separated florets). That is when several florets, each having its own proper cup, are inclosed within one common calyx, so as to form altogether one flower only.

The Syngenesia class comprehends those flowers which Botanists have agreed to call compound. The essential character of a compound flower consists in the anthers being united, so as to form a cylinder, and a single seed, being placed upon the receptacle, under each floret. The Dandelion, the Thistle, and the Sun-flower, are compound flowers, that is, each of these flowers is composed or compounded of a number of small flowers, called florets.

The Cryptogamia class consists of those plants in which the obscure and peculiar fructifications do not fall under either of the preceding distributions; they are divided into five orders.

1. Miscellanæ—Miscellaneous. Including subjects incapable of arrangement under any of the following, and in many respects disagreeing with one another, as the horsetail, &c.

2. Filices—Ferns. A well-known kind of production, comprising plants which have their flowers disposed in spots or lines, on the under surface of the leaves, as in the Polypody and Spleenwort, though sometimes in spikes, as in the Osmund Royal.

3. Musci—Mosses. Familiar subjects.

4. Hepaticæ, a kind of mosses. Distinguished from the foregoing, by a difference in the fructification.

5. Algæ, including plants which scarcely admit of a division into root, stem, and leaf; to these belong the different kinds of Lichens, and Fucus or Sea-weed.

6. Fungi — Funguses. Common objects comprising mushrooms, &c.

" Thus have we given a sketch of the Linnæan division of the vegetable kingdom into twenty-four classes, and of each class into two or more orders.

" The next division is into *genera* or families, each genus uniting together all those plants which bear so strong an affinity as to be considered members of the same family. The name given to the genus is the name by which all the plants of that family are known: thus, the genus *rosa* includes all the different kinds of roses; *salix*, which is the scientific name for willow, every kind of willow; *convolvulus*, every kind of bindweed; and *erica*, all the heaths. The distinctive or characteristic marks upon which the genera are founded, are always taken from the shape, position, number, or some other property of the different parts of the flower, as the calyx, petals, seeds, seed-vessels, &c.; whether they be round, or heart-shaped; whole, or divided; rough, or smooth; single, or many; and the like.

" There is only one more division necessary to bring us down to particular plants. For instance, I have found that my newly-gathered flower is a rose, a convolvulus, or a heath, but I want to know what kind of rose, convolvulus, &c. For this purpose each genus is divided into *species*, the characteristic marks of which are formed upon the leaves, stems, roots, or any other parts of the plant, except the flower; and some name, called the specific or trivial name, is given to each species thus characterized, which, added to the name of the genus, sufficiently distinguishes each particular plant: thus, there is the *salix lanata*, *salix latifolia*, *salix repens*, or the woolly willow, the broad-leaved willow, the creeping willow, and several others, which are all species of the genus *salix*, or willow, in the same way that the long-eared bat, the common bat, the vampyre bat, and the horse-shoe bat, are all species of the same genus *vespertilio*, or bat.

" We have now gone through all the divisions and subdivisions of Linnæus's system of classification for the vegetable kingdom; and have arrived at the ultimate object of our research, in ascertaining the family and species to which any individual plant may belong. I shall now elucidate the whole by an example.

"Suppose that you have found, and brought home from your walk, a delicate, blue, bell-shaped flower, called by some bell-flower, by others Canterbury-bell, and by others again blue-bell. You naturally wish to know by what name this plant is distinguished by the botanist, what name all scientific men in every country have agreed to give it, that you may be at no loss under what name to look for a description of it, or how to communicate to others any observations you may have made upon this plant yourself.

"In the first place, then, examine how many stamina, or how many of those small bodies called its antheræ, are to be found in the bell-shaped corolla, or blossom ; you discover five ; now run over the classes of Linnæus, till you come to that which is distinguished by its five stamina; this is called *pentandria*, and you therefore know your flower to be in this class. Next look for the pistillum or pistilla, of which in this plant you will find only one ; this characterizes the first order, called *monogynia*, and therefore your plant is in the class *pentandria*, and order *monogynia*. You have now done with the stamina and pistilla, and must attend to the other parts of the flower, comparing them as you go on, with the characters of all the genera in this first order of the fifth class. The calyx you find to have five divisions, sharp, and not quite upright; the corolla of one petal, bell-shaped with five clefts, close at the base ; shrivelling ; segments broad, sharp, open ; seed-vessel roundish, of three or four cells ; all which tallies exactly with the generic character of *campanula ;* this therefore is the genus, and you have now only to find out to what species yours belongs. The leaves nearest to the roots, and which are generally so close to the ground as to require care not to leave them behind in gathering the plant, you will find to be round, or rather heart-shaped, or sometimes kidney-shaped, whilst the leaves on the stem are narrow, and strap-shaped; this determines the species, and in this your flower agrees with the character of that called *rotundifolia.* You have therefore now determined your plant to be the *campanula rotundifolia*, and you may read all the descriptions of this plant without a doubt as to its being the same, and may describe to others, where you found it, when you found it, and what else you know of it, without any fear of confounding it with any other blue, bell-shaped flower, of which there are many, both of this and of other genera." See *Skrimshire's Essays.*

INDEX OF FLOWERS.

INDEX OF INTERPRETATIONS.

THE END.